Coffee House Zen
Collected Writings on Life and Spirituality

Scott Shaw

Buddha Rose Publications

Coffee House Zen

Table of Contents

Introduction

Over the years I've written a lot of words about a lot of subjects. At the heart of all of my writings is a person encountering life in the most conscious, helpful, and productive manner possible.

So many people fight their way through their life. They create obstacles for themselves and they hurt other people with the words they speak and the actions they undertake. All of these things create conflict that, in some cases, comes to be the definition of an individual's entire life. Conflict is never a good thing.

It has always been my hope, through my writings, to help people overcome the negative aspects of life, that we all encounter, and transcend to a higher state of consciousness where true happiness and genuine fulfillment may be encountered.

It is hoped, by presenting this collection of essays that were created over the past three decades or so, that the reader will come away with some new ideas, techniques, and inspirations about how to encounter life in a more positive manner while avoiding some of life's obstacles.

Through the writings presented in this book I trust that you will be able to find a new means to encounter your life and from this be able to not only live your own life from a much more refined perspective but be able to pass on good actions and good feelings to the life of all of the other people you encounter thereby being the impetus for a new and a better world.

Remember, all life begins with you. Anything you do has the potential to spread out from you, onto other people, and from there onto the entire world. With this understanding as impetus, I trust these words will help you to become the best instrument of life that you can be and from this do good things that rise outwards from yourself creating a better everything.

Be Positive!
Scott Shaw

I Believe:
Compounding Factual Inaccuracies

Life is based upon a set of beliefs. These beliefs come to us from many sources. We gain them from what we are taught, what we hear and read, what we witness, and then; once we have been provided with a certain set of parameters given to us by our culture, our desires, and our placement in life and time, we decide what we believe.

Some people decide what they believe and then simply do the conscious thing; believe it. Others decide it is they who have the calling, the desire, the ability, the power, the gift, and/or the need to broadcast their beliefs to the world. From this, they spread their ideologies out, from within in their own mind, to others. Why do they do this? The simple answer is ego. They want to be seen as a knower. If they are not seen as a knower then, at least, they believe they will be understood to be a discontent, sewing the seeds of controversy and anarchy.

There is one essential problem is the conception of, *"I believe,"* however. Belief is opinion, it is not fact.

In a free society everyone has the right to have their opinion. But, if a person lives a life of consciousness they understand that their, *"Opinion,"* is just that—it is not a fact. It is simply what they believe and belief is an interpersonal process, it is not a factual accounting of reality and something that someone should expound outwards to the world for then only one thing occurs; the compounding of factual inaccuracies which have the potential to negatively affect the life of others.

It is like the conspiracy theorists, they look for and try to find logical reasoning for what they believe to be an anomaly of life, time, space, and/or occurrences. But, there is fact and then there is theory. Some people attempt to broadcast their theories to the minds of other people. This does not make their ideologies fact; it simply makes them broadcasted theories. And, each theory is simply some-thing that a particular some-one hopes to make fact based upon what they, personally, believe. It is not fact, however, it is simply belief. Yet, they hope to pull others into the web of what they believe. This is how many of the falsehood that have been disseminated through societies, throughout time, have come to take hold. Not fact, simply belief that a large number of people have come to believe.

The fact is, some people are so locked into their beliefs that even if you present them with factual evidence that what they believe is wrong they will argue with you about the validity of your presentation and will not concede that their belief about a practical subject and/or their belief system in general may be wrong.

Some people become very lost between the concept of opinion and fact. If they do not possess an analytical mind they simply assume that there is no difference. People driven by ego, desire, jealousy, or anger often fall prey to their own undefined differences between these two mental concepts. They believe, so what they believe IS. But, is it? Is your belief ever the defining truth for the entire world? Yes, it may be the defining truth for your world but should your belief be expounded to others? Do you ever ponder this fact before you spread your belief(s) outwards?

How much of your life mind-time do you spend pondering the fact of understanding where your belief system arose? How much of your life mind-time do you spend actually contemplating why you are saying, what you are saying, when you are disseminating your beliefs outwards, beyond yourself? When you do speak of your beliefs do you only care about the fact that you desire your beliefs to be witnessed as the truth? In fact, do you ever think at all before you speak of your belief? Finally, what is your desired end result when you propagate your belief? Why do you discuss your belief(s) at all? These are all important concepts to think about as you pass through life.

It is essential to contemplate why you believe what you believe. Think about this, have you ever believed one thing and now you believe it no more? This is the simple formula to help you define for yourself the difference between belief or fact. And, it is also essential to keep in mind, just because other people believe something (even large groups of people like a religion) this does that mean that you are forced to believe it?

Belief is only what it is; an ideology formed in your own mind. As long as it is kept in your own mind, it can hurt no one. As soon as it is released chaos is given birth to.

Belief is never fact.

Surrender

Most people who enter onto the Spiritual Path are drawn to it very early in their life. The majority of these people don't take the steps to actualize their early instincts until they have lived through one too many traumas and are encountering a complete lack of meaning in their life. This explains why there are all the formally depicted reasons for, *"Becoming Spiritual,"* desperation, illness, poverty, loss of a loved one, and so on. Even in the cases when an individual is propelled into spirituality based in those negative motivating circumstances, if they were not touched by the divine early in life, they would not choose spirituality over the more destructive forms of mourning, such as drugs, alcoholism, sex addiction, and crime.

From a personal perspective, defined by whatever unexplained Karma or destiny, I formally entered onto what may be called, *"The Spiritual Path"* very early in my life. I was drawn to Eastern Mysticism as far back as I can remember. As I grew up, in the 1960's and 1970's, the terms: Guru, Karma, Yoga, Zen, and Meditation were commonplace, as were photos of Indian Spiritual Teachers gracing the walls of head shops, homes, billboards, and telephone poles. I suppose being born in Los Angeles, where this type of mindset was much more commonly embraced than in many other parts of the country, didn't hurt to aid in the availability of the spirituality that I came to heartily embrace and allow to formally shape the person I was to become.

Sixteen

When I was sixteen years old, a friend of mine came knocking at my door. I had not seen him in over a year.

We had met when he was a senior and I was a sophomore at Hollywood High School. During our preliminary friendship we realized that we were both drawn to the Spiritual Path. We would spend hours talking about the various philosophies and ideologies of Hinduism, Taoism, and Zen. But initially, we were not able to take the next step and move into the more refined realms of spirituality as neither of us had a car and we had no way to travel to spiritual centers where we could meet the teachers. This all changed a year later.

Post him showing up at my Hollywood apartment that evening, we both progressed into a period of rapid spiritual awakening. We would drive around with Malas, *"Prayer Beads,"* hanging from the rear-view mirrors of our cars, pictures of Krishna or images of the Buddha taped to our dash boards, listening to the music of Ravi Shankar and Bhagavan Das or lectures by Ram Dass and Alan Watts. As we drove we would chant while the passenger played the bamboo flute. We spent the next year or so frequenting all of the spiritual centers along the West Coast. My friend eventually went off to college in Santa Cruz and I found the Sufi Order and Swami Satchidanada's, Integral Yoga Institute. Though I was intrinsically much more drawn to the joy that was brought about by the singing and dancing which served as a meditation tool to the Sufi Order. None-the-less, I found myself spending many nights practicing Hatha Yoga or lost deep in meditation with my new friends at the IYI.

As I look back, I realize how quickly I moved through the ranks of the IYI and quickly found myself in the inner circle of the group with direct access to Swami Satchidananda. This was in no small part due to the fact of my love for Rock n' Roll I had already acquired a vast knowledge about audio taping and how to operate sound systems. Thus, I became Gurudev's soundman—traveling to his lectures, doing his sound, and recording his talks for posterity.

Brahamcharya

It was at one such function in Santa Barbara, where Yogaville West was located at the time, that Swamiji had given a public talk. Though I was a practicing Brahamcharya, *"Celibate,"* and planned to be for the rest of my life, I had brought along this female friend of mine to meet Swamiji.

I had met her at the Sufi Dances and she and I were very attracted to one another. At the time, I believed that if anyone were worth giving up my lifelong plan of celibacy for, it would be her.

Post the lecture, which went exceedingly well, as I was always very conscientious and concerned about the sound being exact, Gurudev returned to his home in Montecito overlooking the Pacific Ocean, and the IYI inner circle gathered at a vegetarian restaurant in Chula Vista—the University town just North of Santa Barbara.

The gathering was coming to a close. It was my female friends and my plan to go camping in the Santa Monica Mountains that evening where our infatuation was leading towards consummation. She and I were preparing to leave when this female Swami came up to me and said, *"My ride has left and you must drive me back to L.A."*

Well, this put me in quite a quandary. I mean, it was getting late and to drive her back to the Hollywood IYI would kill all of the plans my friend and I had in place.

This Swami was a female born on the East Coast and though she had embraced the Spiritual Path she certainly maintained all of the abrupt inner-city traits commonly associated with the East Coast lifestyle. In other words, what she had said to me was not so much a question, but more like a command. I looked at my friend, she at me.

It was one of those moments that seem to go on for an eternity. In that seeming eternity, however, I truly embraced my inner being—that inside place where you simply know. I saw my physical persona, seriously infatuated with this girl, and then I witnessed my pure spiritual being—who knew that if I couldn't step outside of my own desires and help those who needed help, what did the spiritual life truly mean.

I surrendered; I was going to give her a ride home. In that moment of surrender, the Swami's missing ride, reappeared. She had not left, as was suspected. But, had simply gone off to the beach for a gaze at the setting sun. I was saved!

I sat there in the restaurant knowing that it was my surrender, to the situation, which caused Divananda to reappear. Had I fought the test I was given, then my drive down the coast would have included another passenger.

The party broke up with Pranams, *"Prayer Hands,"* to everyone. My female friend and I were in my car heading South—off to the camping spot which she knew of.

By the time we arrived in the Santa Monica Mountains, it was quite dark. And, though we looked

16

and looked, she could not find the camping location. It was decided to give up our adventure. I drove her home to her house in Bel Aire.

The Moral of the Story

We all have the tendency to plan. This episode is the perfect example of the unpredictability of life.

We each set our desires in place and expect them to be actualized. The problem is, there is no guarantee that anything we plan or hope for will come to volition. Not a physical desire, which defined this experience for me, not the enlightenment which is promised at some future date or lifetime to all of those who tread upon the Spiritual Path, not even the assurance that you will be physically alive to experience anything in the next moment.

With this understanding in place, the most spiritual thing you can do each moment of your physical existence, is to surrender to the fact that, *"All is unknown. Nothing is guaranteed."* You cannot know what your next experience will be. You can hope, you can desire, you can plan. But hope, desire, and planning are just that. They are what the definition of those words equal—something that is predicated upon expectation. Expectations remove you from the now. Expectations are as far from Zen as you can get.

Because Zen is only about the Here and the Now.

Surrender

What does it mean to surrender? Surrender is embracing the unknown. Surrender is accepting that nothing is promised.

Accepting that nothing is promised, you are allowed to encounter each moment in its perfection. Encountering each moment in its perfection is the essence of Zen.

Well, though the girl and I remained close for a time, we never had the opportunity to take our infatuation to the next level. She eventually became a Scientologist. Me, I went to India.

Surrender, because in that surrender all is allowed to be as it should be.

A Position of Authority

I think that it is always interesting watching the fervor in which people attack individuals in positions of authority, particularly religious authority. This seems to be a byproduct of this modern, very litigious society that we live in—with its foundations based primarily upon greed.

Let's face it, an attack on any person in a position of authority it is based upon two things. First of all, the person who is on the attack wishes to dethrone the individual they are attacking. They want to make them less in the eyes of others. Why do they want to achieve this? Because they do not believe the individual is worthy—for whatever reason. What their ideology is based upon, however, is ego and insecurity. Why? Because I person who has achieved something in life has no need to behave in this fashion. They have accomplished what they have accomplished, are secure in that accomplishment, and, therefore, live their life from a position of self-worth. Thus, they have no reason to go after another person of accomplishment because they are secure in themselves.

As I always say, you do not have the right to criticize anyone until you have at least achieved what he or she has achieved.

The second reason that an individual in a position of authority is attacked is because the person attacking wants money. They believe that by going after this individual they will somehow remove the wealth they have achieved and put it in their own pockets. They do this, primarily, by suing.

I think that we have all heard stories about people being sued for whatever reason—you particularly hear about these situations when a person has some level of fame or notoriety. Maybe you have been sued?

I too have encountered this style of nonsensical situation. For example, this occurred to me when this one individual, who was lying about his martial arts credentials and was attempting to discredit mine, (an occurrence which is very prominent in the modern martial arts), threatened to sue me for stating that he was a liar. This guy was eventually discredited but, as we have discussed, he tried to make himself more by basing his reality upon lies and attacking me.

Another situation happen to me when a lady hit me with her car when I was riding my motorcycle and almost killed me. Then, she sued me. Of course, she didn't win. But, I mean how ridicules was that?

Another, even more, amusing situation happened to me when a guy came up to me and was attempting to start a fight. Now, I am one of those people who avoids confrontations whenever possible, because they are generally so meaningless. But, just before it got physical, he said, *"You're probably going to beat me up and after you do, I'm going to call the police, have you arrested, and then I'm going to sue you."* At least he was honest. But, this society has gotten so ridicules that you can even go *mano-a-mano* anymore without the threat of a lawsuit.

Whenever I have encountered these situations, I tell these people, go ahead, because at the end of the day, the only people who get rich from lawsuits are the lawyers. And, I just won't play that game. And, besides they would be pretty disappointed in the size of my bank account if they ever saw it anyway… :-)

But, the point I am making is that this goes back to the whole concept of greed, at whatever level. A person who has not achieved anything of importance in their own life, and wishes that they had, wants what another person, in a position of authority, possesses. This is based in an untold number of psychological insecurities and lack of personal achievement.

The ultimate question is, *"What does a person in a position of authority have that other's do not? And, why have they achieved what they have achieved, when other's have not?"* To answer, what they have is the one-pointed drive and focus to achieve. And, this is the primary reason why they have achieved what they have achieved. One the other side of the coin, the lack of this drive and one-pointed focus is what has caused others to not achieve and to fail.

I am not saying that everything that a person in a position of authority does is right—far from it. What I am saying is that what caused them to rise up to their level of socio-economic evolution is, *"Drive,"* combined with a little bit of luck.

Drive is not something you can give a person. Some are born with it. Other's, simply focus their attention to the degree that they achieve what they want to achieve in life. But, once they have achieved this level of success, then they are confronted by those who want to see them fall from grace.

If you ever find yourself in the position of envy or wishing the demise of another individual, you have to ask yourself, *"What does that person have that you do not? And, why have the achieved it, when you have not?"* This is not a complicated question and the answer, if you are true to yourself, should come very easily.

There are positive people in this world and there are negative. It is as simple as that—yin and yang. Some people base their lives on helping others, while others sit around complaining and attacking others when they have no basis to do so. So again, I get back to one of the primary points, *"If you have not achieved what the person you are attacking has achieved, you have no basis or right to attach them, because you are not living on the same level of existence."*

Damages

A lot of people believe that when they feel damaged by a person in a position of authority they are, thereby, owed money. But, what does money have to do with damages. I mean if you get in a wreck, the insurance company of the person who hit your car should pay for it to be fixed. But, once a car has been wrecked, it is never the same. And, this is the perfect example about life. Once something is broken, it can never truly be fixed. It can be bandaged and repaired. In some cases, the scars can be covered up. But, the life is never the same.

This is simply the reality of this place we call LIFE. From each encounter we emerge a changed and different person. Sometime this is a good experience; sometimes it is not. But, the reality of it is, we are changed. What we do with that change is up to us.

Also, many people who are on the leaving-side of a relationship are very bitter. What they wanted, a happy life, forever-and-ever, did not happen. So, they are very angry with their partner and they want to get even. This is particularly the case if the person they were in a relationship was a person in a position authority. They want revenge.

I was just reading about Swami Kriyananda and how he got sued by a couple of his devotees who he apparently had sex with. Now, back-in-the-day, if you wanted to have sex with somebody, you did. And, that was that. You didn't sue them if they didn't answer every need and desire you ever imagined.

I mean, *"Get real people."* You are adults. You can make choices. Just like everyone one else can make choices. If you make the choice to have sex, you made that choice. Nobody forced you into it. It was just a choice you made. If you feel guilty, bad, or whatever afterwards, that is your fault. Live with it! If you are in a relationship, at whatever level, and the other person chooses to leave, that is their choice. People have the right to make choices.

We all make our own choice in life. Some are good; some are bad. Some we wish we hadn't made. But, it is we, individually, who made that choice. You cannot later blame a person and sue them because you are sorry about the choice you made. That is so empty, so irresponsible, and not, *"Owning,"* anything that you have done. It is very unspiritual.

I read so much about this person suing that spiritual teacher, (i.e. the case of Kriyananda), because they had sex with them. Now, I am not discussing the sick priests who mess with young children or the pseudo religious pundits who lead their flock into prostitution or mass suicide. But, in all other cases, you are an adult. You make your own choices. If you later regret being with a person, you have to ask yourself, *"Why did I want to be that person in the first place?"* Probably because they were in a position of authority and it made you feel special that they wanted to have sex or a personal relationship with you.

Own your choices! And, quit trying to make other people pay when they choose to no longer be with you. Or worse…

An extreme example of this is this very beautiful girl who worked as a waitress at a restaurant I used to frequent. I didn't see her for a time and then she returned. Her face was mangled. And, when I say mangled, I mean mangled. Apparently, she had gotten involved with a seedy guy who was really into drugs and he flipped the jeep they were driving in out in the desert. What happened to him, I do not know. But her… She was never the same.

She moved on with her life. As she was a waitress, she had no health insurance and a limited income so she could not afford extensive plastic surgery. Yet, I would see her, waiting her table with a smile on her face. She always seemed happy.

I often wondered how anyone could do that—go back to a place where everyone remembered her beauty and pretend that nothing was wrong. Yet, she did it. Eventually, she got married and had some kids and her life moved forward. If someone can overcome that, who are any of these people to claim some ridiculous, unbearable damage, caused by someone who simply no longer wanted to be with them?

It is like all of the jilted wives (or husbands) of movie or sports stars that you hear about. In their divorce they expect to get all of this money, cars, houses, or whatever from their former spouse. But, why do they deserve it? What did they do that was great or notable? All they did was marry someone and the relationship eventually fell apart. Why should they get half or more or the person's estate? They accomplished nothing. *"Because I put up with*

24

the person," is not a qualifier. That is simply what you do when you enter into a relationship—put up with somebody: good or bad.

It is like the story my teachers, Swami Satchidananda, used to tell. He would say, Relationship are like doing business. As long as you say, 'I love you, honey.' They will respond with, 'Oh, I love you too.' But, the moment you say, 'I don't love you anymore.' They answer, 'Then, I hate you.' But, if love is love then you would love a person whether they loved you or not, no matter what. But, this is not the case, love is a business.

This is the same condition of life. People turn to a person in a position of authority because they like their teachings, their qualities, their success, their whatever... But, just like in love, when they are in their early stages of admiration, they are infatuated and blind to all the faults of this individual. And, believe me, we all have faults; we all have a personality, even the most so-called holy.

So, number one, if you want to seek out a person in a position of authority, understand that they are human, just like you. They possess hopes and desires, just like you. To achieve them, they may build upon their position of authority. If you are willing to give into their desires, that is fine. If not, you have the ability to say, *"No."* So, don't blame them is you say, *"Yes."*

Secondarily, if you have some form of experience with an individual in a position of authority that you came away bruised and damaged from, you must realize that it was your own set of desires that led you into that situation. As such, there is no one to blame but you. Own that fact and quit trying to sift the blame away from your own desires and personal hopes for the outcome of your life.

Finally, if you are on the sidelines and hope to move away from them, you will never be able to base any achievement on the meaningless attacking of a person in a position of authority. All this type of behavior does is to make you look envious, which is never attractive on any level. So, don't do it.

Whether are not you ever ascend to the level of those you either admire or hate is not important. What is important is that you live a life based in the realization of your own perfection. And, attacking people will ultimately negate anything you may achieve.

Yes, you may love this person. Or, yes, may be a little bit jealous about what a particular individual has achieved and think you can do it better. Well, if you can, then do it. If not, then be silent, live your own perfection. Do what you do, to the best of your ability and then all life moves to a much more conscious plane of existence and this world and this universe are left to embrace its own natural perfection.

Are You Aware Enough to Learn?

Life is a never-ending process of learning, expanding, and growing. Life provides the individual with the opportunity to constantly expand their mind, acquire new understandings, while continuing to expand their mind and advance their knowledge.

Not to long ago in world history people were sedentary. They were born into a specific region on this earth's service and, with very few exceptions, they never left. From this, the amount of new information made available to each person was limited. As the industrial age and later the information age came upon us, though a person may never physically travel more than a few miles from where they born, the amount of knowledge that they can readily acquire is mind-boggling. It is all there at your fingertips.

Have you ever met a person who is very set in their ways—very stubborn? They know what they know, believe what they believe, and allow nothing to change their mind. There are many people who follow this mindset. They are proud of believing what they believe and decide that they know enough. They are proud to be firm and in their beliefs and in believing that the already posses all of the knowledge that is necessary for their life. Are you like this? Do you believe you hold enough knowledge? Do you think that what you currently know and the things you believe in it is enough?

In life, you really don't need to know too much to get from one side of it to the other. To pass from birth to death is quite easy if you remain oblivious to all that is going on around you. This is the way many people live their lives. Though this is the way many people live their life, what this does is to keep one from expanding and acquiring the ever-expanding new levels of knowledge, understandings, and consciousness that are now made available to all of us.

In the past, the only way to gain advanced knowledge was at an institution such as a university. This is no longer the case. It is everywhere—available to everyone. Are you taking advantage of this?

Though knowledge is out there in an abundances and many claim to seek it, there is a sub-category of those who claim to seek new knowledge and new understanding but truly are not. This subgroup is made up of people who only seek knowledge that reaffirms what they already believe and/or supports the way they already feel. For this person, new knowledge is not what they are acquiring. What they are doing is that they have already made a choice and then they seek out people, words, teachings, and understandings that support the belief(s) they already hold. Are you one of these people?

Knowledge is based upon two primary conflicting elements: that which expands the mind and gives birth to creativity and positivity and the adverse; knowledge which holds a person bound to a specific belief system where they are not allowed to think freely and are, thereby, driven into the expression of negativity in their life.

The truth is, if you seek out negativity you can find it everywhere. And, the subtle reality of negativity is that it hides in many guises and is taught via many teachings. So much so that few people ever know that negativity is what they are embracing once there are locked into its belief system. Think about it;

does what you currently believe and what you are currently allowing into your mind making you feel joyous, happy, free, loving, giving, and caring? Or, is what you are concentrate upon making you feel angry, angst ridden, fearful, and spiteful? Think about it, what do you think is the better thought pattern?

Though it is sad fact of human existence that negativity haunts the mind of many people, the adverse exists, as well. If you seek out positivity, and will not settle of anything less, it is out there in abundance; it is simply just a little bit harder to find as it does not activate as much adrenaline to hold onto its essence.

What lies ahead of you in life is what you set into motion in this moment. If you open your mind without judgment and you decide to gain new understandings that you may ultimately decide to embrace or reject you can forever learn. If, on the other hand, if what you allow your life to focus upon keeps you locked into a state of stubborn, hurtful belief, and if your study inflicts negative appraisals upon others, then you will be trapped to forever live the same thought patterns over and over and over again.

Life is an ever-growing expansive place. Allow yourself to be a true part of it. Learn, grow, expand.

Coffee House Zen

A friend of mine and myself were at this coffee house in Venice, California last Saturday evening. We were sitting around, taking about life, love, god, and things in general. These two girls came up and sat down next to us. My friend, unattached, became quite exited. This was especially the case when one of the girls leaned over to me and said, *"You look like a Buddhist."* I laughed, because what does a Buddhist look like?

My friend immediately became lost in conversation with the girls. Shortly thereafter, the one who had spoken to me pulls out a cigarette and begins to smoke. She looks over at me, *"I know, I know, a Buddhist shouldn't smoke. I'm bad."* My infatuated friend immediately exclaims, *"Don't worry about it. Do whatever you want."*

It must be understood, however, *"The do whatever you want,"* mentality works fine in the realms of the material world for in that space of perception you can justify your actions and assign them to the mindset of, *"I'm getting what I want. It makes me feel the way I want to feel."* The realm of a Zen is very different, however, as the mindset of, *"I'm getting what I want. It makes me feel the way I want to feel,"* is completely adverse to that of mindfulness.

The definitions of mindfulness and desire oftentimes becomes blurred in the modern world. The reason for this is because of the fact that within the scope of spirituality there are many conflicting teachings. Some tell you that you can only be holy if you adhere to a very strict vegetarian diet, drink only water and herbal tea, associate with only those of like spiritual mind, and so on. Other teachings detail that you can do whatever you want as long as you do it consciously.

Due to these conflicting teaching, many people become very confused on the path to consciousness. On one hand, they know they are drawn to the spiritual path. On the other hand, they are surrounded and influenced by materialism. As such, they are driven to perform decidedly worldly actions and not only find justifications for them, but realizing that they are doing something not good for their body, their consciousness, the environment, or the world on the whole; criticize themselves. None-the-less, the actions are still performed.

This is the place where many people fall off of the spiritual path. Due to the ease in finding associates who do not share the like mind of spirituality, the world draws one to the dark side.

So, what is the person walking the spiritual path, who is surround by the worldly, supposed to do? If we look at life in regard to mindfulness, the question that must be pondered is quite simple, *"Is what you are doing leading you to a higher state of mind?"* If the answer is, *"Yes,"* then the action may be mindful. If it is not, you are not walking on the path to higher consciousness.

As the actions you take in life are always based upon personal choice—the choices you make sets you on the road to higher consciously, universal understanding, a healthier, happier world, and enlightenment, or they do not. Thus, all things that occur in your life; all the people you meet, and the things that you decide to do in association with those people you meet—all of the outcomes that occur due to the decisions you make are based upon one single choice. What is your one single choice? As that one single choice will come to define your life.

Consciousness

Zen is a pathway of consciousness. The more consciously your live your life, the more direct your path towards spiritual realization.

Defining Consciousness

People on the Spiritual Path commonly talk about consciousness. But, what is consciousness? Many believe it to be some mystical state that can only be achieved by an ancient sage after years of meditation. This type of definition removes consciousness from the realms of the here and now. It makes it something distant and unobtainable and provides the framework for all kinds of justifications why you cannot become conscious, Right Here, Right Now.

As human beings, schooled by this modern world, we have, in fact, been guided away from consciousness. There are an untold number of distractions, self-orientated philosophies, and teachers who guide us towards selfishness, but not consciousness.

Consciousness must, therefore, be redeveloped by each of us. This is accomplished by transcending the limitations of learned physical existence and evolving to a new level of universal awareness and understanding.

The Bathroom Detail

When I was sixteen or seventeen I was asked to accompany a fellow disciple and professional electrician, whose spiritual name was Bhagwan, to the Montecito home of our guru, Swami Satchidananda. I was to assist in the installation of our Guru's jacuzzi. Though I had spent a lot of time in the presence of my Guru, I had not been invited to his home. So, I was obviously filled with an untold amount of youthful exuberance.

Bhagwan and I arrived early in the morning and spent the day working on the jacuzzi. Occasionally Swamiji would come out, check on our progress, correct the logistical mistakes he thought Bhagwan had made, and occasionally make joke with me or pat me on the head. He was obviously amused that I was much younger than the majority of his disciple. I was still in High School...
This personalized interaction was, of course, a higher honor than I could ever have hoped for at that point in my life.

As the day concluded, we were scheduled to travel a few miles up the coast to Yogaville West, were Swamiji was to give a talk to his disciples. As we were a bit dirty, our Guru invited us to use his personal bathroom to clean up. This was a blessing of an unparalleled degree. When I later related this fact to the other disciples, their jaws all dropped in disbelief that we were allowed to use the Guru's bathroom.

Bhagwan was the first in. He took seemingly forever. I sat on Gurudev's bed, anxiously waiting, knowing that Bhagwan was taking way too long. When I finally was allowed in, the bathroom was a mess. Bhagwan had left dirty water all over the sink, the dirty towels he had whipped his hands with were thrown haphazardly on the ground. I couldn't believe it! I immediately got to work cleaning up his mess. Approximately two minutes into the job, a knock came upon the door and Swamji's secretary said I really needed to hurry up, as Gurudev needed to get ready. So, I had only a moment or two to finish my clean-up of Bhagwan's mess and to wash my own hands.

I exited none too happy with my spiritual brother. I mean, how could he do that? Make a mess and leave it for me to clean up. And, he made me look I was the one taking way too long...

I was very young and naive so I keep my opinions to myself, as he was in his early thirties with a family and a job. But even then, I understood conscious verse unconscious actions.

Not to be critical of any individual, but we all possess our own set of foundations. Me, I was taught that you should not make a mess in someone else's house. Bhagwan, even though he possessed the outward appearance of walking the Spiritual Path, obviously had not learned the same lesson—nor had he opened himself up to the level of consciousness where you take other people into consideration.

The First Step to Consciousness

You must begin at the beginning. The first step on your path of consciousness begins with your foundations—with what you already know.

You must study yourself and detail how you have learned to act and react to situations. For example, what would you have done if you found yourself in the aforementioned situation? How would you have naturally reacted?

Once you have defined these areas of your personality, you must consciously decide if they are right or if they are wrong.

Each of us will find areas that appear to be fine and other areas where we know we need to change. This is the point where you make your first conscious decision to make the person you are into the more universally conscious person you hope to become.

This is not necessarily easy. For we have all learned how to react certain ways—encounter specific situations with a particular attitude and interact with people in a prescribed manner. For the most part, this education never took place in a formal manner. We, as children and young adults, learn how to treat people and encounter situations from those around us. In many cases, we learned from people whose lifestyles were in complete contrast to consciousness. Thus, you must focus and motivate your own change.

Change does not occur overnight. It must be practiced.

This is where your first formalized steps into consciousness take place. You must decide to alter an area of your own personality and then do it.

If you slip and retreat to your old patterns of behavior, don't beat yourself up about it. Simply realize that you are on the Spiritual Path. The Spiritual Path is a step-by-step road to realization. You are now taking the initial steps you need to becoming the more conscious individual you know will emerge.

Keep in mind, that this preliminary step to consciousness is essentially important. For without a complete internal assessment, you can never hope to truly know yourself. You will simply pass through life reacting unconsciously to whatever situation you may encounter. This is the most animalistic level of human evolution.

Without knowing self, you can never transcend self. Transcendence requires that you know what you are ascending from and where you are ascending to. Thus, knowing you is the first step of refined consciousness.

R. Buckminster Fuller

When I was an undergraduate at California State University, Northridge, I observed another interesting occurrence, which delineated varying levels of consciousness. R. Buckminster Fuller, one of the greatest analytical minds of the twentieth century, came to speak at my campus. The hall was stuffed beyond capacity and they were not allowing anyone else to enter. I was not willing to be turned away, however, so I eventually found my way up to the second level mezzanine where the spotlights found their source. From there, I could see and hear him fine.

He began his talk at about 12:30. A little before 1:00, half of the audience began to get up and leave. He asked, *"Where are you going?" "To class,"* was the answer, which rang from the mobile audience. *"Why are you going to class,"* Bucky exclaimed. *"They have nothing to teach you. But, I do!"* Unfazed, the exodus continued.

I was standing there in disbelief—nobody even knew what Bucky was about. He was just a name and a lecture to attend during lunch.

For me, this optimized the perfect example of unfocused consciousness. You do something for the doing, with no mental content.

The lecture proceeded with half of the auditorium empty.

The Second Step to Consciousness

The second step to consciousness is to consciously perform all actions.

To focus your consciousness you must make all of your actions as precise as possible. This is how all of the great spiritual teachers have truly given something to this world.

As long as you do not think or do not care, your acts will forever remain simply unconscious actions. Unconscious actions only cause reactions.

If you wish your acts to transcend the limitations of this material world, you must do whatever it is you do from a perspective of pure one-pointed consciousness.

Doing things conscious is not as easy as it may sound. For example, think about the brown rice you prepare. When you wash your rice before you cook it, do you ever allow a few grains to fall into the sink and be swept away? If so, think about this next time you are hungry. How many of those grains of rice, that you have unconsciously let slip away, would it take to fill your stomach?

This is obviously simply an example. But, if you wish to enter the realms of true consciousness you must do everything you do in a very refined manner.

There will always be mental justifications to forgive yourself for the unconscious actions you take if you allow yourself to accept them. If, on the other hand, you choose to live a life of consciousness, those justifications can never be embraced.

The Third Step to Consciousness

The next step in ascending consciousness is you must ask yourself, *"What are you doing with your life?"* If you cannot answer that question, you are not walking the path of consciousness. Thus, you must take the time to sit down and define what is going on around you. Formally designate what has taken place in your life and what has led you to where you are today.

The best way to do this is to actually write it down so it is in front of you in black and white and can be studied. From this, you will gain perspective. From perspective you can conclude how you have ended up where you have ended up. Thus, you can chart the next step in your life from a place of consciousness.

Once the first question is answered, you must then ask yourself, *"Why you are doing what you are doing?"* Because without formulated reasoning, what you are doing is simple what you are doing. It is not performed consciously.

Nobody can tell you why you are doing what you are doing. Not religion, not astrology, not your loved ones. You are you. Each person is based in a secular consciousness. You have lived what you have live. These factors have defined the person you have become. Before you can transcend the limitations of self, you must know who self is.

So, at this point, acutely detail why you are doing what you are doing. You may like what you find. If so, then nothing needs changing. If not, then you must be the one to consciously make that change.

The biggest mistake that people commonly make at this stage of life analysis is that they decide they hate their job, hate their mate, hate their life and they throw it all to the wind. This is not consciousness.

From a perspective of consciousness you make changes to your life consciously. You chart out your actions, how they will affect others, and then you move towards a desired end in a slow controlled manner. From this, you do not damage the lives of others, nor do you leave yourself destitute.

The Forth Step to Consciousness

This is the stage where you begin to formalize your spiritual pathway. Though you have no doubt been walking the Spiritual Path throughout each of the previous stages, at this point you formally make it the defining element to your life.

Many people believe to do this that they must leave the material world behind and move to an Ashram or go to India, Nepal, Thailand, or Japan. This is incorrect.

Going is only going. Though you may have new experiences, you may even have fun, going is not the pathway to consciousness, as going is based in desire.

In Zen we understand that everything you need to find spiritual enlightenment is Right Here, Right Now. Going only takes you away from the here and the now. Thus, going never leads to Nirvana.

To become consciously spiritual, is to accept.

Life is life and there will be trials and tribulations. Many people falsely believe that they should not happen to a spiritual person. Yet, they do.

Embracing truly conscious spirituality is about accepting the perfection. Knowing that all is as it should be. If you want things to be different you are only embracing a mindset bound by desire.

The consciously spiritual person understands that by letting go of desires, they will be joyous at any life occurrence, as they will see it as a pathway to further refinement of consciousness.

Consciousness Unconsciousness

There are some people who walk the path of spirituality and place reasoning behind their unconsciousness. They provided seemingly poetic statement to justify their unconscious actions. *"I am just doing what I am doing—simply a leave which has enter the stream of life and am flowing as nature guides me."*

Yes, you can place a leave in the stream and, yes, it will flow until it reaches the ocean or is stopped by some obstacle. But, does it care that it is flowing in the stream? No, it does not. It is simply flowing the path that was laid out before it, with lack of consciousness.

To consciously enter the stream of life is very different from unconsciously ending up in the stream of life and ending up wherever it is you end up. This is why you must take control and refine your consciousness.

The refinement of consciousness can only begin with you. Ultimately, consciousness is how you interact with this place we call life. Consciousness is the thoughts you think, leading to the actions you take. Consciousness is what you do and how your do it. Consciousness is your choice.

Choose to live consciously and Nirvana becomes obvious.

Evolutionary Choice

Throughout the evolution of human consciousness there have been a lot of saying and/or slogans that have been spoken. Some have come to be used over-and-over-and-over again. From this, they have come to be believed metaphors. Near the top of this list is the saying, *"You only get one shot."* Meaning, you only get one chance to make something of your life, but if you don't, it is all downhill from that point.

Think about it. How many times have you heard that saying or a similar one?

Many people say it. Many people believe. But, is it true?

Choices

We all make choices in our lives. Sometimes we choose to go this way. Sometimes we choose to go that way. The reality of choice is, however, once a choice is made, it sets the next set of evolutionary choices in motion in your life.

For example, sometimes we make a choice and are so happy with the outcome. In other cases, once we have made a choice, we realize that it was a very bad choice and we should have followed a different path. But, the choice was made. And, by making it, it has come to define the next set of circumstances in our life.

Life is made up of choices. It is as simple as that. Some choices we make we will be very happy with. Others, we will wish we had not made.

But, this is reality. This is life.

No one is happy with every choice that they make. But, choice is one of the most dominant factors of human existence.

Choice and Desire

The choices we make are predominated defined by desire. We want something. We want a desired outcome. We want a desired object. So, we make the choices we believe will allow us obtain that object.

The problem is, until you have obtained that desired object you never know what owning it will mean. Whether that object is a thing, a person, an occupation, or a level of achievement—until you own it, you can never truly understand what the choices you made to get it will equal.

This is kind of like the American folklore analogy of the bluesman who travels to the crossroads to sell his soul to the devil to become a famous musician. They sign the contract, they get what they were promised, but the outcome of fame is completely different than they thought.

This is like life. There are all kinds of subtle costs for obtaining any desire that can never be anticipated. Thus, many people are left realizing that they got what they thought that they wanted, but now they no longer desire to pay the costs and be defined by their original desire. But, it's too late. They already made their deal with the devil.

In life, we all want things. So, we go about obtaining them. Once we get them, however, we often realize that their ownership is not at all what we had anticipated.

For example, someone meets a person and falls in love. They enter into a relationship with the person but then it all goes bad. It ends, and they are very sorry they ever met or desired the person because of all the negativity that the relationship has cost them. This same scenario goes onto employment goals, possessions, and everything else.

The reality is, you cannot know what a desire will equal until it is lived. And, once you live it, it may destroy you. But, you made the choices to get to that end-goal. So, who is to blame?

Choice and Reality

Choice is one of the subtlest components of life. And, all choice are not as all-encompassing as the previously detailed ones. Choices are also driven by life necessity. For example, someone makes a choice to go to the supermarket. They get in their car and get in a car wreck. A choice; yes. But, it was defined by an unanticipated outcome.

This is the other reality of life in association with choice. There are a zillion people, animals, objects, and acts of nature that can never be charted or anticipated. They exist in their own sphere of reality, just as you do. So, while you are doing what you do; so are they. And, the two of you may come into unexpected contact. This is life.

Circumstances

As stated, what a choice does is to set the next set of circumstances of your life into motion. Your choices cause your evolution. And, good or bad is what you make of the outcome of each choice. But, good or bad is not wholly defined by you receiving a specific desired outcome.

As I have long discussed, it is you who decides what to do with the life circumstances you are handed. It is you who decides to become held back and hindered by them or to learn from them, and move forward. Like I say, *"If you love Hell, it becomes Heaven."*

This being stated, in life, you must make choices. These choices will be fueled by your desires. And, do not get it wrong; even the most spiritual of people have desires. Desiring god-consciousness or nirvana, that too is a desire. So, as material as your desires may be, they are no less holy than that of the monk. They are just desires. Desires are just a byproduct of life. And, these desires will set your life in motion by the choices you make to obtain them.

Whatever happens is whatever happens. A choice turning bad or transforming into a believed opportunity missed does not need to define your life. What defines your life is what you do next. And, *"Next,"* is available until you die.

Here is the reality. You get a lot more than one shot in life!

Higher Consciousness: A Study in Fiction

Since the dawning of advancing consciousness, people have put forth the idea that you can advance your consciousness, you can become more, superior, and/or enlightened. At the core of all of these teachings is separation. By seeking higher consciousness, you are becoming more than the person next to you. They are of a lower mind because all they think about is their desires, their car, their house, their family, their whatever... But you, the seeker, you are more! You are something different—someone more holy because you are on the path to higher consciousness.

This trend, this definition, has been taught a thousand different way throughout the various religious traditions and spiritual schools across the centuries. There have been a few teachers who have stepped to the forefront of the pack and have expounded new and somewhat different teachings. And, for whatever karmic reasoning, they have been remembered throughout history. Schools and religions have been created around their name. Siddhartha Guataman, the Sakyamuni Buddha, Jesus, Mohammed, Sri Shankaracharya, and the list goes on. Then, there have been the teachers who reference these individuals as supreme beings. Many of these teachers devote their entire lives to, The Becoming, of what these teachers propagated and the higher consciousness they were believed to have possessed.

But. Let's step back for a moment. *"What is higher consciousness?"* What do you define it as? What do your teachers tell you it is?

The first step in understanding higher consciousness is defining what it is to you. Because what it is to you, may not be what it is to me.

The next question you must ask yourself is, does pursuing higher consciousness actually make you something more, something better as has been laid down throughout time.

No one can tell you the answer to those questions. I can say, that if we look at the masses of humanity, we can see that most people pursue nothing more than the fulfillment of their own momentary desires. They want what they want. But, I want what I want to. You want what you want to. And, the person seeking higher consciousness wants what they want; namely, higher consciousness.

Ask yourself, *"Is the pursuit of higher consciousness any different from wanting a new car, a new girlfriend, a new boyfriend, a new watch, or a new whatever?"*

Certainly, there is the belief that a person on the Spiritual Path is not so much seeking things only for themselves but are more set upon a course which is designed to aid in the betterment of all of humanity. For example, there is the, *Bodhisattve Vow,* where a person makes a vow to gain enlightenment for the benefit of all sentient beings and once they have achieved enlightenment they will continue to reincarnating, (continue to come back to this place we call life), until all of humanity is fully enlightenment. That sounds selfless. But, is it?

If we take a more refined look at this concept, it brings us back to the primary point, *"What is the key concept in the Bodhisattve Vow?"* It is that one

47

person will do one thing. They have heard of it. They desire it. So, they pursuit it. Thus, it is nothing more than a desire.

Though the spiritual practitioner may make it sound like they are doing something for the good of humanity, we still come back to the central focal point of, *"I." "I will do this. I will get that. Then, I will do this for you to make all things better."* Me, me, me...

Can there be any concept of, *"Me,"* and, *"I,"* in true higher consciousness?

Some spiritual traditions teach that their techniques cause a person to loose all sense of, *"I."* But, this is also one of the main selling points that has been used in the propagation of the use of hallucinogenic drugs, *"You will lose yourself. You will become one with all"* But, this is all mumbo-jumbo. It is simply a means and a method of convincing people that there is some strange and illusive cosmic thing out there that they cannot encounter naturally.

To the matter of fact; yes, some hallucinogenic drugs will cause you to lose your sense of self. But, then the drug wears off and you are back where you started. The only problem is, the drug has altered the chemistry of your brain forever and you are never the same. And, that, *"Never the same,"* is not a good thing. Or, the drug has altered your brain to the degree that you become mentally ill. In this modern time they have developed some pharmacological drugs that can help reverse this pattern. But, nonetheless, you will be left with, *"Never the same."*

If we look at this ideology a bit deeper, *"What do you become if you have no sense of self?"*

Again, here we are taken into the rhetoric of higher consciousness. It is often stated that, *"This person's consciousness is so high that they are completely removed from self and are completely removed from this world."* Well, so is a person who is insane. Are they enlightened? Have the achieved higher consciousness? Immediately the argument will be made that they did not choose their condition but a holy man did.

Choice is a condition of life. We all choose what we choose. And, for the most part, people who want to be something, oftentimes pretend that they are just that; whether they are or not. They fake it till they make it.

"Oh no, my guru isn't like that!" How do you know?

Most people never have the opportunity to spend enough one-on-one time with their teacher to truly see that they have human flaws. They are simply allowed to see a presented image. Moreover, if one follows a, *"Supreme teachers,"* who has passed away then all ability to see who they truly were is long lost, as they died a long-long time ago.

All if this is not to say that there is not true spirituality. And, this is not to say that there are not those who truly possess higher consciousness. But, how many times have you found yourself thinking, *"Oh that teacher is a fraud. He or she is not truly holy."* How many people have said that about your teacher or about you?

As there is no one definition, there can be no one higher consciousness. Since there is no one higher consciousness, like all things it life, its pursuit is left to the definition and the belief system of the individual mind. What you believe may be completely disavowed by the person sitting next to you. And, in fact, a few years down the road, you too may completely believe something different than you do today.

Belief is only that; belief. It is a perception individually held by each person. It is not universal. As it is not universal, there is no one way to attainment. There is only YOU and what YOU believe.

What do you believe and why?

Karma Consciousness
or the Consciousness of Karma

You have done something that has hurt someone but instead of understanding the pain you have inflicted you think about yourself.

You have taken something from someone but instead of understanding the loss you have created in the life of that other person you think about yourself.

You have lied to someone but instead of understanding the confusion and chaos your expressed falsehood has created in the life of that other person you only think about yourself.

You have spread rumors behind the back of someone but instead of caring about the damage you have done to the reputation of that person you only think about yourself.

If you ask anyone why they have done what they have done that has hurt or altered the life of another person they will always provide you with a reason for what they have done. But, is that reason the truth? Though it may be the truth that projects from their own mind, their mind only thinks about themselves. Their mind is only concerned with themselves. Ask the person who was affected in a negative manner by what another person has done and they will have a completely different perspective. Whose perspective is the correct perspective and based in the absolute truth?

There are always two sides to any interpersonal equation. There is the person who is the instigator/the doer and there is the person who is on the receiving end. The moment that doer sets a course of events into motion that hurts another person in any manner they become the criminal but how many people think of themselves as a criminal. They may think of themselves as the victor. They may think of themselves as the winner. They may think of themselves as the controller. But, they never think of the other person as anything more than the adversary, the diminished, or the one they have conquered.

People raise themselves into life defined by a desire to become. People raise themselves into life defined by a desire to have. Ask yourself, what is becoming? What is having? What is any accomplishment or win in life defined by if that personally defined achievement takes from the life of someone else? But, who thinks about this? Who thinks about their impact? Who cares about their impact? Who cares about anything or anybody as long as they have gotten what they want?

Have you ever observed a person who is at the top of their game? Have you ever watched a person who is at the top of their profession? Have you ever watched a person who is flush with cash? What do you observe? Is the person caring or giving? Is the person extremely conscious of those they have climbed over to get to the top? Is the person cognizant of what they have done to get where they are? Or, do they only relish in their own power and become very angry when someone challenges that power? And, if someone does, what does that person do to that person? Do they care about them? Do they understand them? Do they give to them? Or, do they find a way to attempt to diminish that individual?

Observe a person who has done something that has hurt someone else. Now, observe that same person when something is done to them. Who do they think about? Do they think about the person or people they have hurt? Or, does all focus shift only to themselves as they blame the person who has counter attacked?

People never think about the pain that they caused other people. People never think abut the karma they are creating. People are selfish. Why do you think there is so much chaos in the world? Why do you think there is so much pain in the world? Why do you think there is so much conflict in the world? The answer, people only care about themselves. Thus, giving birth to a never-ending stream of karma.

If you want to know who a person truly is, observe how they think about, talk about, and treat other people. If you want to know who you truly are, observe how you think about, talk about, and treat other people. Who are they? Who are you? And, do they/do you treat people the way they should be treated?

If you want to see where your life will end up. Study the way you interact with other people. Observe they way you speak about, think about, and treat other people. You define them as they will ultimately define you. You set your own destiny into motion. Be the source of caring.

Lose Your Identity, Erase Your History

The majority of people desire to become SOMETHING. Early in their life they see those who are respected for doing what they do and follow the path of seeking that same admiration. Ask yourself, *"Do you seek to become nothing, to be seen as nothing, to be unknown? Or, do you hope for something more for YOURSELF?"*

People do all that they can to achieve. Though most never find the pathway to find their ultimate dream, they, none-the-less, try to rise to a position of respect and authority within their place of employment, in their community, or at their school.

Most people eventually find the road to marrying and having a family. At that point, the focus of their life quite often shifts from desires for Personal-Self to desires for their child and/or children. *"I want the best for my child. I want them to have a better life than I have had."* How often have you heard those words spoken?

Having a child is not a bad thing. Having desires for one's child is not a bad thing. In fact, having a child often takes the egocentric focus off of the individual allowing them to rise from a life of self-centered thinking to a life of caring and giving. How many of the people you have met, who do not have children, are truly caring and giving people? Most, are simply lost in a Life-Pattern of selfish thought, thinking only about themselves.

Life-Patterns are instigated by the individual. What one does now leads to the next set of available options in one's life. As such, the desire(s) that are

54

pursued defines the entire evolution of a person's life. Though desires may change and what a person does may set a new course of options and availability into motion in a person's life, everything you desire, and everything you do to gain that desire forever defines your life, as your life is one continuous emulation of whom you want to be leading to what you are.

Think about the actions you have taken to achieve your desires and your dreams. Have they hurt anyone? Have they hurt you? Are you proud of them? Do they make you ashamed? Do they make you happy or do they make you sad? Remember, you wanted something, you went about achieving that something, thus, it was you who set your ALL into motion by wanting what you wanted, desiring what you desired, which means you are personally responsible for all the goodness and/or all the damage you created in that pursuit. If you hurt anyone in that pursuit you will be forever bound to that person as you did what you did and their life evolution was changed because of it. Remember that.

The thing about personal achievement is that most of the achieved have not cared about their personal effect. They only think about themselves and achieving their desire and thus, the thought of damage to others rarely, if ever, comes to mind. As much as the person of consciousness will say, *"This selfish mindset is not the attitude one should possess,"* this has been one of the key traits of humanity since its evolution to the realms of thoughtful-self. People only think about themselves and what they want!

Now that this has been established, let's turn this scenario around a little bit. What if you desired nothing? What if you wanted to be nothing? What if you did not care about your position or your legacy? How would you be feeling right now? What would you have done differently in your life? What would you not be regretting? Who would you have not hurt? Who would you have not been hurt by?

If you did not want to be something, if you did not do the things you have done to be that SOME-THING how would your life have evolved differently?

The fact is, in life we can never go back in time. We never get a re-do. But, what we can do is to become conscious enough to look deeply into the patterns of life and learn from not only our evolutionary movement but the evolutionary movements of all those around us. We can open our eye.

If you can take a moment and step away from yourself and your desire(s) long enough to truly witness what is going on with your life, the lives of those you interact with, and the lives of the Greater-All, then you have the chance to become more than your limited, selfish self. Instead of possessing a desire for your life to be some idealized ego-driven machine, adored by the masses, you have the chance to truly do something good for the world by becoming something that no one else can see or worship, a True Being not driven by ego and desire.

Most people don't want this. Most people don't understand this. Most people if they heard about it simply dismiss it as nonsense. They do this because they are so locked into the realms of their own identity, of their desire to become what they desire, that they are too lost to understand that they will never achieve what their mind sees. Why? Because what is, *"Out There,"* is never *"In Here,"* it is all an illusion. What you see other people BE-ING is never what you can BE because you are not them, just as they are not you. What you see out there is a projection of an idealized reality you have fantasied in your mind. It is not real. At best, it is only what you hope it will be.

By comprehending this you allow yourself to realize that all that you hope to be, all the steps you take to get there, are, at best, simply your projected desires where you attempt to live a reality that may never be had. Thus, your desires to BE are nothing more than a Self-Instigated Illusion.

Knowing this, you have one of two choices to make. …Two choices that now you can make very consciously. One, are you going to continue on the path you are on, doing what you are doing, damaging who what you are damaging? Two, are you going to let go and simply BE? By being, you become free. Your desires are let go so you create nothing: no bad, no good. From here, you can be happy and whole within yourself. From here, no one is hurt, thus, you are not re-hurt. You are complete free and not trapped by the hurt that arises from not having what you want.

Freedom is always a better perfection that a life bound by desire. You are you. YOU is all YOU will ever be.

Do you want to be happy in your freedom? Or, do you want to be tormented by what you desire?

Lying to the Liars

I believe that we live in a very interesting time in that anyone can become a celebrity overnight. Say or do something on the internet and if people find it interesting it can spread worldwide. A truth or a lie it does not even matter, simply by saying it and/or doing it, your words and your actions are out there and there are those who will believe every word that you have spoken. Thus, the world is no longer based upon fact, it is simply based upon what someone has said.

I think back to a friend of mine I met a few years ago. She was a young girl working as a barista at Starbucks. All was well with her world. She had met a guy, had fallen in love, and she was beaming that she was in a relationship. A few months go by and her boyfriend breaks up with her. Then, the guy begins to tell the personal story of their relationship online; attempting to make himself look more manly and her look bad. He begins to spread lies about her on *Facebook* and *Tumbr*. First, she is destroyed... A beautiful young girl who had been shunned by her boyfriend. She would call me up trying to find solace. I would help her as best as I could. Then, the lies began to be believed by others who read them. She told me how she would get messages from people she never even met reinforcing what her ex had said and they were condemning her. This, even though every word he wrote about her was from his own personal perspective and/or was a flat out lie.

The outcome... First she got fired from Starbucks because she came to working hurting from what her ex and his internet cronies had said about her. Then, she took her own life.

I believe that most of us have enough positive people in our life who would help us and support us if and when people hurt us and/or if somebody began to tell lies about us on the internet. But, then there are those who do not. Sadly, this girl was one of them.

Have you had people tell lies about you on their internet? I have.

I certainly understand that my position is a bit different from many. For better or for worse I have, through many-many years of hard work, accomplished a few small things in life. From this, some people have come to love me, while other have come to hate me. Why? That is all based upon their own personal psychology.

The thing that I have realized is that those who are the most vocal on the internet are those who are the most insecure and negative in life. A secure person is whole onto themselves and thus they do not need speak about anyone. They do not need to write nonsense on the internet. Love a person or hate a person it does not matter as they are whole onto themselves—they are doing what they are doing, pursuing what they are pursuing, and that is the focus of their life. Their life is not based upon other people.

The fact is, a secure person is busy pursuing their own dreams and they do not need to reference others in their quest to achieve them. It is, however, the insecure person and/or those who are not something onto themselves that must continually reference others. They must talk about others. They must write about others. They must make comments about others. They must try to hurt others in the eyes of other people. They do this because they are not something. They are not whole onto themselves. For ultimately what is the purpose of saying negative things about anyone? What does it prove? How does it make you any more or any better?

If I think back to the friend I lost, there she was this young, in love girl, damned by someone who obviously did not deserve someone so caring as her. Yet, what he did set an entire course of destiny and karma into motion because he was not adult enough to simply move way from a relationship that he no longer chose to be in. And, look at what occurred. Look at what were the consequences of his actions.

I believe we each have heard stories about similar situations on the internet. From that, I believe that each of us truly needs to take a look at who and what we are and how we behave on the internet.

Do you attack people on the internet, hiding behind a screen name or even using your own name? Do you spread your particular side of a story on the internet about a person or a thing? If so, why? Why are you not enough to care more about another person than yourself? Do you believe that you are so special that you do not need to care about other people first?

The ultimate truth of life is we are only as good as the words we have spoken. We are only as good as the deeds we have performed.

Life is based upon what you have done. What have you done? Have you cared more about yourself and your feelings than you cared about others? Have you cared more about what you have wanted than what others have wanted? And, mostly, what have you done? For what you do is a choice and what you do sets your everything into motion. If all you think about is you, if all you think about is how you feel, if all you think about is how others see you and think about you then your life is lost. You will never be what you hoped you would become because you have hurt others. And, there is no justification for hurting others by your words or your deeds; especially if your words are not based in the truth. It is especially importation to note that this means not just your personal interpretation of truth but absolute truth.

In closing, it is far better to keep your words, your opinions, and your emotions to yourself—especially in this day and age where everything you write or say (on the internet) can have such wide spanning effects. If you hurt someone by your words, if you spread your personal opinions about someone, if you tell lies about someone, there can and will be consequence. If you set something in motion you are responsible for those consequences. Think about it.

Meditation is Everywhere

Traditionally, a practitioner of meditation is taught to remove themselves from all external sights and sounds. Most forms of meditation teach the meditator to close their eyes and ignore all sounds that they may hear. Personally, I have long believed that meditation is everywhere. Instead of running away and forcing yourself to pretend to not hear sounds, you should embrace them and make them part of your meditation.

Most people now live in urban environments. In the cities there is a constant barrage of sounds. Not only are there the sounds of nature, such as wind, rain, birds and the like, but there are also all the sound of man: cars, airplanes, construction, and people talking.

Attempting to turn your mind off and not hear those sounds is very difficult. This is especially the case for the individual who is new to meditation. They sit down and they try and try to not be distracted, but the sounds take them from their meditative mindset. Then, as they have become distracted, then mind finds its way to think— thinking about all the things the mind likes to think about... But, if you take a different path of meditation, if you allow the sounds to become part of the process, then meditation becomes much more natural.

For example, when you initially sit, it is always a good idea to calm the mind through a few deep breathing exercises in order to gain a certain Center, and refined sense of control over the Self. Once you have done this, you can allow your mind to become focused much more easily. Then, instead of running away from your environment, embrace it. If a car drives by, remain focused; by follow its sound as it drives off into the distance. If some someone is pulling their suitcase or bag on wheels, listen to it rumble across the pavement. If you hear a lawnmower in the distance, allow its motorized rhythm to capture your mind and hold it fixed. If you hear a siren, embrace its sound, study it, and come to understand its essence as you listen as it fades off to the distance.

In both urban and natural environments, there is the sound of nature. Obviously, the sounds possessed in nature tend to be much more constant and soothing than those of the city. But, they too can be no less jarring to the meditative mindset if you try to turn your ears off from hearing those sounds. So again, when you sit to meditate and you hear the sounds of birds chirping, wind blowing, the ocean or a river flowing, instead of hiding from it, embrace it. Allow it to become a part of your meditation. Let the sound guide you deep into the overall essence of nature. Become a part of it. Understand and embrace it.

Being what you are, where you are, who you are, while fully taking in and merging with the source point of the energy that is surrounding you is the ultimate form of meditation.

On the Inside Looking Out

When one thinks about those who walk upon the spiritual path, the idealized image of an individual wearing long robes with a shaved head or a sadhu with long dreadlocked hair and an unshaven face is commonly the first thought which comes to mind. These external images of apparent holiness sets those who live in the modern world to somehow believe that an individual is not truly holy if they wear normal clothing, shave each morning, and get their hair trimmed one a month.

When I was an adolescence, forging my way on the spiritual path, I sent a letter to the modern American guru, Ram Dass. I posed him a few questions, which my adolescence mind believed to be very important at the time. Though I was not sure that someone so seemingly holy as Ram Dass would have the time to send me an answer, a month or so later, a reply did, in fact, come in the mail. Yes, a letter from the man himself. As I read his handwritten words, I found that it was not just a reply but I also received a personal invitation to meet with him at a gathering he had scheduled in the Los Angeles area the following month. My youthful mind was awh struck.

The day of the gathering arrived, and I made my way to the location. I walked into the room and there he was, Baba Ram Dass, the man who the media had made mythical. I was somewhat set back, however, as he came up to happily greet me. I realized that he wore common slacks and a pull over sweater. Somehow, I had expected him to be wearing the traditional clothing of a Yogi: a dhoti and a kurta. Or, at least, the cotton drawstring pants which were commonplace for the era. I mean, all of my friend on the spiritual path wore pseudo Yogi clothing. Why didn't he?

This erroneous mindset is the perfect example of that possessed by many of this modern era. Holiness is gaged by external appearance. By how a person looks, not by how they live. It is for this reason that so many people play, *"Dress up."* They somehow believe that if they wear the robes of a monk, have the dreadlocks of a sadhu; that if they appear holy, they must be holy. But, this is all folly.

There is an amusing story which details the other side of this issue and describes how a person who is not walking the spiritual path perceives one who is.

When I was in my third semester of college, I had already long been living the spiritual lifestyle. As such, I had been initiated into the order of sannyas and was wearing the orange clothing that delineate my standing. (Not orange robes, just orange clothing).

My collegian friends would just call me, *"Swami,"* as most of them couldn't get their tongues around the longer version of the spiritual name I had been given. They were all supportive of my path, however, commonly asking questions; as strange as I may have appeared.

I was taking a class on philosophy, which at that time was my major. The instructor was an aging professor, who was one of those people who projected the mindset that they knew everything and the students knew nothing. He was obviously much different from my previous college instructor on the subject of philosophy who was a Vietnamese Buddhist monk.

We took our midterms. Though academic Philosophy is about as far from the root source of the word as one can get, I, none-the-less, believed I had done okay on the exam. When the tests were returned the following class meeting, I was presented with the grade of *"F."* Down the side of my paper was a paragraph long discourse on why I had received the grade. *"You cannot be a Swami, you are too young. You do not know enough. You will never know enough. You are Caucasian, not East India, etc., etc., etc..."* There was, however, no comment on my actual essay answers.

At the time, this attitude shook me. Having surrounded myself, from a young age, with those walking the spiritual path or those who were my close friends and were very accepting of my chosen vocation, I had never encountered this style of prejudice.

The grade I received made my classmates quite angry, however. Much more angry than me, as I was locked into the pseudo spiritual space of, *"It all is as it is. It is all perfection..."*

When I left the class that day, I wondered how I was even going to pass the course if I was to be judge by how I looked, not by how I performed. This brought to mind the questioned that had been posed to me many times, *"If I was walking the spiritual path, why even bother attending a university?"*

For me, education was about learning for the sake of learning. Though being spiritually innocent is a benefit, being uninformed seems to serve little purpose. Though the established educational institutions are certainly not the only pathway to schooling, for me it seemed the appropriate road.

As I walked across campus mentally debating the occurrences of the day, I thought back to a time a year or two the previous—I was going to the store to buy some supplies for a spiritual community I was involved with, the Integral Yoga Institute. I was standing, waiting for the light to change on Sunset Boulevard in West Hollywood, when these two girls from the Midwest drove up. Seeing my long hair, long beard, prayer beads, and funny clothing, they asked, *"Are you a Hippy?"* I laughingly answered, *"No, I'm a Yogi."*

When I returned to the center, I told my story to one of the sisters of the order. She said, *"See, God was testing you."*

On the spiritual path you make a choice everyday. You can choose to follow the ways of the world. Or, you can choose to follow the divine order of the universe and be spiritual.

This understanding certainly has nothing to do with how you are dressed, however. But, how dress will delineate how you are perceived.

The Sikh wears a turban. This tells the world of their religious conviction. The Priest wears a collar. This lets everyone know of their profession. But, does what a person wears truly depict spirituality? No, it does not.

External is always external. External can never be internal.

What you wear for clothing can tell the world something about the life you choose. It can even influence how you behave—if you are seen as holy, you may behave in a more spiritual fashion. Though all of this may be seen as an aid to spiritual progress, in actuality, it truly is not.

External image also leads to ego. The monk who wears robes is immediately assumed to be and treaded as a holy crusader, just as the military officer who wears a uniform is immediately seen to be a trained combatant and is treaded accordingly. To truly embrace spirituality, you must transcend the need to be defined by your external image.

The modern teacher, Bhagwan Shree Rajneesh, though he became seemingly lost in the power of his position as his years as a teacher progresses, his original teaching, none-the-less, possessed a very pure understanding of universal suchness. He believed that if a person wished to renounce the world, even for a moment, he would provide them with the method to do so. This was the basis for what he called, *"Neo-Sannyas."* And, explains why he had so many followers who wore orange clothing and possessed the title of Swami.

This ideology is very true. If you can simply renounce the world for a moment, the rest of your life will be altered for the positive. If you can let go of your desires: let go of caring who you are, what you are, what you are to become, and how the world perceives you, even for a second, then in that moment of freedom, you can touch Satori.

It is essential to remember that spirituality is not defined by what you wear or who you are on the outside. Spirituality is about who you are on the inside.

It took me awhile, but I left behind my orange clothing. It took me a little while longer and I left behind the Sanskrit names and the yogi clothing— though this was not before I received a *"D"* in the class from my all-knowing philosophy professor, who was the perfect example of the fact, perception are the basis for *maya.* And, *maya* is the pathway away from *Satori.* As long as you care about how you are perceived, you cannot perceive your true Buddha Nature.

Let go of perceptions and the world will be a much better place. Let go of excuses; forget about how a person, situation, event, or even yourself appears. Move past the external, embrace the essence of nothingness. This is Zen.

Simplicity in life is a complex paradox, with seemingly never ending disagreements, differing opinions, dissenting philosophies, emotional manipulations, and even physical confrontations. Some people seem to not only instigate this adversarial mindset but also appear to actually thrive on it.

One may assume that if they walk away from the world and enter onto what is commonly known as the *"Spiritual Path,"* they will no longer be subjected to conflicts and encounters. Unfortunately, the predominance of the world's population is not made up of individuals whose minds are focused on the spiritual elements of life. In fact, it is so common that we encounter people who are willing to do whatever it takes to gain whatever moment of gratification they desire that modern society has given them positive designations: *"Motivated," "Driven," "Hungry,"* or *"A Goal Seeker."*

More than being simply an external social phenomena, many people find that they are constantly at odds with themselves—continually robbing their own inner peace. *"I shouldn't be doing this," "I'm so bad," "I can never succeed,"* and *"I'm unworthy,"* are just a few of the examples which ramble constantly through the minds of many individuals.

We can easily understand that certain people may have developed a negative self image due to childhood trauma, economic or emotional destitution, interaction with unsavory people, or being psychologically manipulated and guided down a negative road by an unworthy dominator. But, why

70

don't these people immediately leave behind this disruptive inner dialogue the moment they realize it is robbing them of their tranquility?

Some people believe that if they could go someplace else, do something else, then they would know peace. But that place is not here. That action is not now. Thus, it is forever someplace else—where the grass promises to be greener. What commonly occurs, if a person relocates to a new location or takes on a new lifestyle or employment position, is that they are no more satisfied, fulfilled, or peaceful than they were before the move, which they believed would change their life.

Some individuals realize that they possess a lack of peace and wish to change this mindset, so they look to the lives of ancient spiritual masters, believing that their teachings hold the truth to contentment and enlightenment. Though this is a generally held belief, it was not always the case. For example, if we look at the historical foundation of Zen, we see that in the Seventh Century C.E. the monk Hui-neng defeated his Master, the Fifth Patriarch of Ch'an Buddhism, Hung-jen, in a spiritual poetry writing competition. As he won the contest, he believed that it proved he was more enlightened than his teacher. His teacher was not so pleased and set about on a course to destroy his onetime disciple. Because of this, Hui-neng had to flee the region. Though this action was instrumental in giving birth to the Northern and Southern schools of Ch'an Buddhism, which eventually lead to what is commonly known today as Zen, it clearly illustrates that not even the ancient masters were free from competition and conflict.

Conflict is a part of life. If you allow your peace to be taken away from you by external occurrences or internal disharmony, then you will never know contentment.

Peace is an inner triumph. It is not something which someone or something can give to you. To embrace peace, in all life situations, you need to develop the skills to become like the calm in the eye of the hurricane—peaceful in a world torn by conflict.

The Foundations of the Pathway to Peace

To begin on your pathway to peace you must ask yourself, *"What would bring me peace right now?"* Would it be a certain amount of money? Better employment? A new place to live? To be in a relationship with a specific person? Maybe to be ten years younger? Perhaps to be more beautiful, thinner, or taller? Or, to be enlightened?

Step One

Your first step to Peace Realization is to consciously understand—anything which you do not currently possess, anything you are not right now, does not exist in this moment. As long as you choose to hold onto the desire of something you do not currently possess or something you are not, you will never be at peace. You will continue to torment yourself with the desire of attainment. This is not to say that you cannot move forward with your life. But, you must do so in a manner where you embrace the here and now. You must decide to love each moment for what it is, and then move forward in a state of peace, not a state of disharmony.

Disharmony is contagious. Disharmony is addictive. It is addictive because it provides the body and the brain with a constant source of adrenaline. It is invigorating. But, it is not healthy. Remember, peace can also be contagious and addictive. Peace, however, is not only better for the person, but better for all those who inhabit this place we call life.

Step Two

As long as you choose to believe that something outside of yourself will bring you peace, you cannot experience peace. Let go of your desire and peace will surround you. This is not to say remain stagnant. Instead it means love each step of the way. Embrace the moment and love each experience you encounter in this moment. It may not be what you desire, but it is, nonetheless, what you are living. Embrace it, whether you like it or not, and peace will find you.

Step Three

Know that the essence of peace is not outside of yourself. Understand that it is in you. Take a moment and find that place of peace. Begin right now. Close your eyes. Let your mind stop racing. Allow your inner guide to take you to that place in your body where peace emanates. For some, it is their heart center. For others, it is the third eye. Wherever it is for you, go there and embrace the totality of peace—even if just for a moment.

Do this several times a day. Come to know this place. Understand this experience. Then, whenever you find your mind torn by desires, when you are attacked by the negative energies of others, or when you find yourself lost in desire, hating your current moment—go to this place in yourself and find peace.

Reality and the Spiritual Path

Just as in the concept of enlightenment, many people believe that by walking the Spiritual Path they will somehow be removed from the trials and the tribulations of life. Certainly, with a spiritual mindset, most will possess a better set of tools to deal with reality than the average person who fights their way through life dominate only be desire and the fulfillment of those momentary desires.

This being stated, the reality of life is, you will encounter obstacles, even if your feet are firmly planted on the Spiritual Path. This is the reality of life.

Some people choose to believe that when they encounter some form of reality, that they are not particularly happy with, they are being tested. But, this is just mental nonsense—justification for the reality of reality.

Why would anybody be testing you?

The simply fact of the matter is, life is life. There are so many people doing so many things—all based in their won desires, that is factually inevitable that you will encountered someone or something that will cross your path and challenge your peace.

I often detail evens that have taken place in my own life to illustrate this fact. The fact, that we all encounter Life-Things that we do not like. No one is immune.

And, the more you are out there in life, the stronger the chance of these events occurring we be. This is why some of those walking on the Spiritual Path choose to retreat to monasteries and live a life sheltered from the world. For within those walls, the chances of being forced to deal with the reality of reality are far less possible.

Personally, I too have spent time in a monastery, locked deeply within the walls of a religious group. One of the first things that shocked me was that I quickly came to realize that there were personality conflicts within these groups, as well.

At the time I came to realize this, I was sixteen years old and full of all of the youthful exuberance of someone newly walking the Spiritual Path. Though it shocked me at the time, it also caused me to realize that this is the reality of life and particularly life on the Spiritual Path. No matter how much you attempt to run and hide to be spiritual, the reality of life, ego, desire, and the definitions of humanity will come to find you.

It is important to understand that this is not bad or good. It is simply life. And, in life we are all destine to deal with Life-Stuff. So, running and/or hiding is never the answer. Sure, it can be nice to get a break from the daily grind. But, it will never free you from the Human Condition.

This being said, the ultimate truth is that all you can do is live your life as spiritually and as consciously as possible. When Life-Stuff comes at you, do what you can do to keep your focus on the spirituality—keep your gaze focused on enlightenment and try to gain new realization while learning from the experience(s). Perhaps you will learn a method to keep you from dealing with that same type of experience ever again.

The reality of life on the Spiritual Path is that we all must realize that we are no different, certainly no better than anyone else. All we are is someone who embraces the seeking of higher consciousness and attempts to make sense of the actions that take place in this place we call, *"Life."*

So, when something comes that you don't like... ...And, it will come. Stay conscious, step back from the emotions that surround it, (especially if they are negative emotions), and embrace the essence of who you are—a spiritual being.

Waste Not Want Not

It's kind of interesting, I just had a new faucet put in my kitchen and all of sudden there is a very powerful force of water coming out. It wasn't like that before. It was normal. Now, it is actually powerful.

I'm sure you people out there who know a lot more about plumbing than I do would know the reason for this. Me, I'm just an observer.

The thing I quickly came to realize with this situation is, that before when I would fill up a pot or a coffee pot or a whatever with water it was very natural. Now, so much water is pouring out, I really feel like I am wasting it.

You know, I am one of those people that does not want to waste resources. I really try to keep my usage of everything check. I really try to stay conscious. I have seen too many situations around the world where people are in need and though we live in the land of plenty I really try to keep my mind observant about what is going out. I do not want to waste!

So, I guess this is my new meditation. ...To be in control of the water in my kitchen. Like I always say, Meditation is everywhere. It is simply what you choose to focus your mind upon.

Change is always interesting. It always makes thing change. If we just stay conscious through the moment of change than maybe it can lead to our next realization.

Like the old saying goes, *"Waste not, want not."*

Where Does Your Empowerment Come From?

Each person wants to exist in a world where they are liked, loved, well thought of, and even respected. They want to be cared about and they want to have their life mean something. To achieve this, people go to all kinds of lengths. The problem is, these lengths are commonly defined by less than ideal actions. From this, though a person may, at least temporarily gain some of the something they desire, it eventually falls away because it was not a life constructed upon consciousness, thinking of others first, and caring about humanity more than one cares about themselves.

Take a moment and think about the various things you have wanted for your life. Look at what you want now. What are you doing to receive it? But, more importantly, think back to what you wanted one year ago, five years ago, ten years ago. Did you receive those life-things? If so, what was the price of you getting them? How did you getting them affect others? And, once you got them did they truly make you a better, more whole and happy individual?

This is thing about time; it allows us to gain perspective.

In life, there is one common problem. That problem is, most people think about themselves first. They only care about other people in so much as they affect them. Obviously, this is a very selfish mindset. But, this is how much of the world

78

operates.

Think about this, how many times has someone only been thinking about themselves and your life or your life evolution was negatively affected by their behavior? Now think about this, how many times have you hurt someone else's life by you only thinking about yourself and you did not even care?

Right now, take a moment. Think back one day, one month, one year, or five years—think about another person that you interacted with. Focus on them instead of yourself. Think about how your own self-involved, selfishness affected them. You probably didn't care then. Do you care now?

If you live your entire life based in a space of self-absorption you exist in a very selfish realm of consciousness. The fact is, many people don't care. They justify their actions. *"I am doing this to get that." "People have hurt me so I have the right to hurt them."* But, more then these mentally verbalized excuses; most people are so lost into the realms of the selfish-self that they do not even take the time to take others into consideration. They do what they do. They do what they do and at best they make up justifications and/or excuses for their actions. But, the fact is, the moment another person has entered your life, either by choice or by fate, you are forever intertwined with them. Anything you do that affects them, affects you. And, though you may gain what you want for your life in any given moment by exhibiting bad or selfish behavior, it is that behavior, in and of itself, that will eventually cause you to lose the thing you gained and/or not achieve your ultimate dreams.

Think about life. Think about the people in your life. Think about the people that you actually know; not someone that you have heard about. Think about these people because by looking at them you know what you know; it is not some abstract rumor, thought, or impression. Think about these people. How many of them are truly happy, truly fulfilled, have truly obtained what they have wanted from and for their life? For most of us, when we actually take the time to take a conscious look we will see that most people are unfilled and have not achieved their whole and compete dreams. This is simply a fact of life.

Again, look at these people. What have they done to get where they wanted to be? In their process whose life did they damage in a small or a large way?

From any damage comes further damage. The damaged go on to damaging others. Why? Because they have been hurt. From this hurt they feel they have the right and/or the need to hurt others. *"It's been done to me."* But, this is biggest excuse that many people employee and the entirely wrong space to live your life from. This is a space of expounding the negative in life; not the positive. If you consciously set about on a path to hurt, by saying bad things or by doing bad things to any other person, your life will forever be defined by those actions. This is why most people never live their life dream. They are held back by their thoughts, words, deeds, and actions.

Many people, however, do not knowingly set out to damage the life of other people. But, they do not take conscious action. They simply do what they do without conscious thought. Is this style of behavior then forgivable because it was not consciously set in motion? No, it is not. For if you go through life lost in your self, locked in your own mind, then by that very thought process you have committed the ultimate sin—you only thought about yourself instead of the great whole.

People lie. People cheat. People steal. People deceive. People hurt other people; whether consciously or not. People lie to themselves about what they have done. People justify what they have done. People do all of these things to get what they want. But, if getting what you want involves the damage of anyone or anything you will never truly get what you want. If you do, it will only be very short-lived. And then, you will have had it but will suffer from the losing of it.

If you are not thinking about others first, if you are not putting other people first, you are living your life from a very selfish mind-space. From this, all that is born is disaster. Be more. Care about the other person first. From this, a whole new world of internal achievement is given birth to.

Try it out. See how it feels.

You Are Not a Christian

I was the only customer shopping in a small boutique. There were two employees in the shop having a heated discussion. I could not help but overhear their words. The one, a man, was stating that he believed that it was the fault of the immoral policies of the United States government that had unjustly imprisonment suspected terrorists at the prison at Guantanamo Bay and due to the harsh conditions they were forced to undergo, with no hope of a fair trail or release, that it was the fault of the United States government that some of these prisoners had committed suicide. The female employee argued that these people were simply mentally ill and, if they were not, they would have not committed suicide. The argument went back and forth with no end in sight until the man said, *"Well, if you believe that, that means that you're not a Christian."*

Throughout all levels of society this type of statement comes into play when a person is not getting their way in a conversation and/or argument. It is kind of like embracing the philosophy of, *"Well, since you won't agree with my point of view, I will simply kick you below the belt, to get my point across."*

Why is this style of dialogue added to a discussion, because from this style of rhetoric, the topic completely changes. The female employee exclaimed, *"What! I'm not a Christian! No, you're the one who isn't a Christian!"*

Ultimately this is the sad reality about opinions that equal discussions that ultimately lead to arguments—people what to talk. They want to say what they believe. They want their point to be accepted. They want everyone else to embrace their philosophy. And, they want their opinion to be accepted as RIGHT by the masses. When it is not, then the rules of discourse go out the window and it becomes everyman (or women) for themselves.

Why Participate

The ultimate question you have to ask yourself is, *"Why should I participate in this style of discourse at all?"* Certainly, throughout life, we have all disagreed with what other people have said. For example, I was recently at a party in Orange County California. For those of you who are not familiar with that region of the country, it is commonly understood to be a bastion of Caucasian Republican conservatism. I was sitting with a couple of friends at a table and a person came up, sat down, and blatantly began to state as fact that the reason gas prices were going up again was because it was a secret plan of Obama. I said, *"No, it is because of world market demands and the speculation of investors."* Another person chimed stating that he was expecting Armageddon to occur any day now because Obama had been elected president and Obama was destroying the way the world views the United States. In disbelief I inquired, *"What do you think W. did?"*

The two ultra conservatives began to exchange agreeing banter. The three liberals, myself included, got up and left the conversation.

We Each Have Our Opinions

We each have our opinion. Some of our opinions are based on fact and some are based in belief. But, most people already have their minds made up about what they do and do not believe. It is for this reason that, for the most part, intellectual discussions among people of differing mindsets rarely prove anything. For example, try to argue with a Christian, detailing the facts of the true history of Christianity to them, and you will run into a brick wall of denial of facts. First you will be told, *"It is all based in faith. And, faith is what our lord expects of us."* Then, if you still carrying on the discussion, you will ultimately be told, *"By the way, you know you are going to Hell for being a nonbeliever."*

This life-fact of differing opinions is the basis for all elements of conflict. So, first and foremost, before you even enter into one of these heated discussions, you have to decide, are you will to entering into a conflict. If you are, you must first understand, that conflicts only end one way—there is a winner and there is a loser. Now, the person of war may be willing to pay this price and live their life by this standard. But, this is emphatically NOT the spiritual way. The spiritual way is a path of peace and positivity—though so many so-called spiritual people forget this fact when attempting to defend their ideology.

But, the debative conflict of life is much more subtle that this. At the heart of all debate is the ideology of one person who has instigated the verbal confrontation. From that one person, the debate grows and grows and grows. But, no matter how big it gets, it is based upon the ideology of one person. And, what that person is propagating is most commonly based on attacking the thoughts and actions of another person or person(s).

Schadenfreude

It is somewhat like the German term, *"Schadenfreude,"* which can be translated in several ways but basically it refers to the fact that a person or persons takes joy in another person's demise or fall from grace. People who embrace this mindset look down upon the accomplishments of another and, in fact, find accomplishment a reason and motivation to denigrate and criticize people.

For whatever reason, people love to congregate in their own negativity. They love to band together and find a place where their voice of negativity can be heard and embraced. Some may say that this is a human condition. But, I don't believe that to be the case. The only reason that a person or person(s) may relish the demise of another is based in the fact that a negatively-based person has not achieved the level of accomplishment or success they have desired in their chosen field. Or, if they have achieved a certain level of success, they feel that by bringing another person down they have become superior. But, higher and lower is all foolishness. Less or more is all a state of mind. And, less or more, higher or lower, is never a concept embraced by the truly spiritual individual.

From a personal perspective I have seen this many times. Someone will contact me being very friendly—most commonly based upon the fact that they want something from me. Then, sometime later, I will find that this same person is speaking or writing very hash things about me, most commonly based upon lies and falsehoods.

Why do people choose to behave in this fashion? Because that is the mindset they have ultimately chosen to embrace. They have entered a space of negativity. And, this goes on throughout the world constantly. Think about it, how many people have you heard speaking negatively about someone they do not even know and have never met? The problem with this mindset and reaction based mentality is all that it produces is a nonsensical waste of LIFE TIME and LIFE ENGERY.

The question to ask yourself, if you find yourself embracing a negative mentality is, *"Do you feel good when you criticize others? Does it make you a better person? Does it make the world a better place?"* The answer will almost universally be, *"No."*

What behaving in this manner actually equals is that you are not contributing to the Greater-Good of this place we call Life. Instead, if you are following this negative level of human consciousness, you are not contributing to the betterment; you are only trying to destroy. And, destruction on any level is a negative pathway.

Think about the people you have admired. Do they follow a path of negativity or do they provide the world with a positive service? Think about the people who have made major contribution to the world. Are they negative and critical? Are they constantly involving themselves in criticism, arguments, and negative debates? No, they are probably not.

No matter what field they are in, what they do is to do what they do. They continue to learn and grow as an individual, and follow a path that leads to the betterment of the themselves and the world. They turn away from confrontations; verbal or to there wise. This is the path to making a positive contribution to the world.

So, you enter into a space where people are embracing negative dialogue—either about a subject, a person, religions, politics, or whatever. Do you stay and take part in that? Argue your point until you make everybody believe as you believe? Does your dialogue continue until you are both so agitated that you end up in a physical confrontation? Or do you walk away? You must understand that if you remain in debate, all you are actualizing is the revamping of meaningless banter and discourse. Yes, you may have your opinion, based on fact or fiction—we all do. Yes, you may like or dislike a person who is in the spotlight, based it whatever ideology. But, as long as you are taking about them, all you are doing is adding to their notoriety. It is kind of like the fact that Andy Warhol never read the reviews written by his critics; all he did was measure how big the printed discourse was.

What this means is that you are either becoming you and becoming more. Or, you are not. If you are not, and constantly engaged in debate that all you are doing is basing your life upon the actions and achievements of other people.

You can be an armchair quarterback and talk, blog, or write, (good and bad), all you want about another person or another person's philosophy. But, if you are doing this, all you are actually doing is paying tribute to that person. And, if you are following this life course, then you must ask yourself what does it equal and how it is causing you to become more, better, and achieve what you truly desire?

So, argue if you want. Stay in the debate if you must. Hit below the belt if that is the only way you can win an argument. But, ultimately what does that say about you? And, more importantly, if you live your life at this level, what will be left when you have exited this place we call Life. Will you have left a positive legacy? Or, simply a plethora of forgotten conversations based on opinions.

Zen Conscious Interaction or Interaction Consciousness

Life is about consciousness. Life is about consciously living. The more consciously you live your life, the more refined understanding you develop about the inner workings of yourself, humankind, the universe, and god.

Most people spend their entire lifetime driven by unchecked emotions and desires. They run from wanting to anger about not getting what they want. When they get, they are happy for a moment but then they want something more and from this they are no longer content. Thus, they are again driven to disharmony and rage about not having all that they desire. Though this is a common thread that runs through the life of many/most people, this is the ideal example of a life defined by lack of consciousness as there is nothing conscious about desire, wanting, and rage.

Everyone wants what they want. This is an element of the human condition. This being said, the consciousness individual, the person who walks the path of consciousness, does not let desire and/or emotions control their actions and reactions to the world around them. For if you do, that means you believe yourself to be the center of this universe, which you are not. If you do live your life by this code, however, by doing so, you do whatever you deem necessary to get what you want. But, by living your life in this manner, you injure the lives of all those around you. This is never the path of consciousness.

Many people are falsely feed the belief that if they ask for forgiveness, if they do something good, then their wrongs are righted. No, this is incorrect. Yes, at some point an individual who has wronged others, driven by the own emotions and desires, may experience remorse for their actions, but the only doing is the undoing of anything bad you have done but this is impossible in this Life Space. What you have done is what you have done and though you may seek forgiveness for your actions; your asking forgiveness from a religious elder or some divine entity never can change what you have done. Thus, the person, persons, or the Life Space you have damaged, remains damaged.

People wanting gives birth to lying. People wanting gives birth to damaging actions. People wanting gives birth to bad behavior. People wanting never gives birth to refined consciousness.

In this world people seek. They seek possessions, they seek position, they seek power, some even seek enlightenment. But, the common factor and the incorrect element to this equation is, *"The seeking."* For at the very root of seeking arises the desire for things to be different than they already are. At the very root of seeking is born the concept of unhappiness due to not having. From this, all the damage to others, all the damage to the earth, all the damage to the all and the everything is given birth to.

At the root of Life Betterment is consciousness—focused human consciousness. As humans, all we can be is humans. As humans, we are defined by being human. This being said, it is the person who chooses the path of refining their consciousness that consciously eliminated as many of the negative obstacles of human existence as possible; namely: uncontrolled desire equaling rage, equally lying, equally power-grabbing, and power-tripping. From this, the damage unleashed onto others is minimized and the world becomes just a slightly better place.

Zen Mindfulness and Can You Remain Mindful When the World is in Chaos Around You?

There is the old adage that it is easy to be holy if you live in a monastery. It is much more difficult to be holy on the streets of the modern world. In addition to this statement being very true, it is also an important factor to keep in mind on your path to mindfulness.

Born in Los Angeles, California, I have been drawn to the spirit of the driven mother ocean as far back as I can remember. Due to this calling, I have lived near her shoreline for virtually my entire adult life.

Having lived in a particular area of Southern California for many years, I would occasionally stroll past this one particular expansive condominium building on my evening walks and think, *"What a perfect place to live. How will I ever be able to afford to live in that building?"*

As if a jokingly given gift was presented to me from the great beyond, a few days after my mother left her physical body, I was looking though the newspaper and found a unit for rent in the building. Though not cheap, it was affordable. Ecstatic, I applied, was accepted, and moved in.

Looking out of my windows I see the expansive Pacific Ocean. Listening, I continually hear the sound of the divine mother's waves.

Though a seemingly idealistic environment, the building is inhabited by a large number of very wealthy people, including an infamous African-American television evangelist who during the

1960's and 1970's milked an untold number of elderly people out of their life savings—promising heaven if they contributed, hell if they did not. Hand-in-Hand with this affluence comes a definitive problem; the individual units of the building are continually being remolded: floors retiled, carpets torn up and replaced with hardwood floors, design alterations, rooms expanded, and so on... Whereas most of the inhabitants leave for their plush offices or on shopping sprees early in the A.M., before the constructions gets underway, I am left bombarded by a seemingly nonstop barrage of sawing, pounding, and generalized annoyance.

Perhaps the most telling thing about this situation is that during periods of silence, I fall in love with my surroundings. Then, each time I have a project to complete, it seems new construction begins. Thus, I am kept from the peace and solitude and seemingly forced to the necessity of mental focus to the degree where my creativity can be channeled while noise constantly rattles my concentration.

Initially, I became very upset at the noise. I would blame people's desire and vanity, (including my own), karma, god, and anything and anybody else around me. *"How can I be creative with all this noise,"* I would scream.

Somewhere along the pathway I realize, however, that you cannot be reliant upon silence if you wish to remain mindful. Mindfulness cannot be defined by a quiet, passive environment. You must be able to focus your mind to the degree that you can transcend the limitations of the physical world. If you cannot do this, your life, and particularly your mindfulness, will be constantly controlled by your external environment.

Though the noise continues, even as I write these passages, I have been able to create some of my most important work, to date, while living in this building and living through all of the construction turmoil. At some future time, I may move away from this building. For now, I use it as a karmic guru, teaching me to transcend the domination of the material world.

If you choose to walk the path of mindfulness, you must do the same. For if you are only mindful when things are going the way you want them to go, you are not mindful at all. You must be mindful in noise, in chaos, in traffic jams, and in the midst of a heated argument. To do this, you must develop the ability to step back from yourself and remain free of judgment in a world dominated by individualistic desires.

Stepping back, seeing the truth in the chaos, and the perfection in the absurd, this is Zen mindfulness.

I Know More Than You

This place we call LIFE is a curious phenomenon. In association with all of the unwanted events we have to deal with; be they natural catastrophes, lying politician, or just the generalized reality of the unwelcome things that happen that we don't want to happen—we must also deal with other people. And, this is where LIFE gets really interesting.

How many times have we each encountered someone who defines themselves as better or more than us simply because they believe the life they are living is somehow more accomplished, more worthy, or simply superior?

"I am better than you because I don't eat meat, I don't drink coffee, I don't drink alcohol, and I do yoga!"

Or, *"You are a sissy because you don't eat meat, don't drink, don't take drugs!"*

These individual rationales continue:

"I know more than you and because I went to a better university than you!"

"I live in a better neighbor than you do."

"My race is better than yours!"

On the spiritual path this style of nonsense occurs, as well.

"I can meditate longer than you."

"My religion is the only true religion of God!"

"My teacher is more holy than your teacher!"

"You practice cowboy Zen. I am a practitioner of REAL Zen!"

"Jesus is the only true way!"

And, the martial arts, (oh my god), it is saturated with 'Better than you' judgments.

"Your style sucks! My style is superior!"

"Your techniques are terrible. My techniques are so much better!"

"I know the real history of the martial arts, you don't!"

"I can kick your butt! Let's fight!"

Who of us has not encountered this style of, *"Better Than You Judgment?"*

Now, it is NOT simply that these people are out there and we happen to meet them. In many cases, we invite these, *"I'm Better Than You"* people into our lives. For example, people who practice psychology are some of the worst proponents of judgment ideology. What's worse is that they are provided with the license to do just that.

The problem is that even though people who study psychology may be doing what they are doing from a perceived perception of service, they are basing their assessments upon their own set of reality—not upon what is the TRUTH. They judge a person by what they've been taught or have come to believe is the TRUTH—delineated by what they perceive they have come to know about a specific individual. But, the reality is, no one can ever truly know another person. They are simply being provided with a distilled set of experiences.

The fact is, even in psychological settings, people only reveal what they want to be known about themselves. Even if the patient is telling a psychologist the truth about themselves, as they believe it, this truth is dominated by personal ideologies, emotions, and gained understandings. Thus, it is not the TRUTH, as any relayed experiences are dominated by the individual's perceptions and understanding about a specific set of circumstances and about the other people who inhabited that set of LIFE circumstance. This is why psychology is a very flawed science.

Many psychologists are schooled to believe that they have some key to other people that the rest of us do not possess. But, a psychologist only possesses a very limited amount of information about the true psyche of any specific individual. They only know what they are told. And this, in most cases, leads to more problems than it solves. Nonetheless, by being awarded a degree, a psychologist is provided with a basis for *"Accomplishment Superiority."*

"What happened in your childhood to make you feel like that?"

"You're experiences are based in insecurity"

"Maybe you need to change your life?"

But, this is all memorized psychobabble rhetoric. And thus, their options, though based in qualitative statistics and appropriate schooling, are no more valid than the individual who claims superiority based in a completely animalistic sense of SELF.

Spiritual Judgment

Spiritual Judgment holds its own unique set of criteria and is perhaps more damning than any other. I mean as soon spirituality or religion is involved than God comes in to play. And, when God is active, then all of the promises or curses of Heaven and Hell are in motion. And, due to the childhood programming instilled in most of us born into the western culture, mess with God or his servants and we are screwed.

How many times have those who hold the power in spiritual circles told people to do something and those people then believed it simply because they were told the speaking individual was a vessel of God and what they spoke was the words of God? To hear this, you may say, *"Come on. I would never believe that kind of nonsense!"* But, look around you. How many people that you know go to church, belong to a religious study group, have become Buddhist, Muslims, Born Again Christians, whatever... Simply because they were seeking a more fulfilled life and a connection to God or the Buddha?

The fact is, people are lost. They seek interpersonal interaction with others. And when the promises of religion come knocking at the door, they jump at the promises.

Many of these people become a part of the religious society for a time and then fall away. Others become deeply involved and become Priests, Swamis, Nuns, Monks, Yogis, or just generalized members of a cult.

Now there is nothing wrong with any of these things. This is your life, and you can do whatever you want with it. Society may tell you a cult is bad. But, if it makes you happy, who is really to say that what you are doing anything wrong?

It is simply that at this level of personal interaction, *"A Member"* begins to hand their life over to the person or persons in control. And, by doing that, one relinquishes control and thereby removes them self away from the path to true inner self-knowledge. This is the case, even though most religious group detail that one must TOTALLY give themselves over to the leader if they wish to truly interact with God and the divine aspects of this universe.

But, isn't any leader of a group simply dominate by the *"I am more than you mentality?"*

I AM MORE!

At the heart of unconscious human existence is the need to be more, excel, overpower, criticize others, and teach. Somehow in modern society the BIGGER are always defined as the BETTER.

Many will say, *"Well that is the way of the world."* And, they are right. One would think that by being spiritual, however, there would be a way to step back from the controlling worldly-hands of power, control, judgment, and the need to be MORE. And, to a certain degree there is—one can go deeply into their mind, withdraw from other people, and completely remove themselves from this material world. In fact, this is why yogis have gone off to caves since the beginning of time; to remove themselves from the ways of the world.

This escapist ideology has always presented a problem, however. Because by escaping you may, in fact, come to control your personal mind. But, life is designed as an Interactive Sport. And, this is particularly the case for those who walk the spiritual path.

What this means is that not only must you find a way to come into harmony with the spiritual energies of the universe and nature, but also with man. (And, I use, *"Man,"* as a generic term). The problem is, with people there is judgment and conflict and the ideologies that MORE is always better.

Individual Creatures

We each are very individual creatures. We each have grown up in unique environments with unique personality traits, born form an individual set of experienced experiences. From this is born individual opinions, desires, and the way we each view and define the world.

Again, one may claim that simply by moving into a world of spirituality you can remove yourself from the controlling hands of the world to the degree that one can overcome these defining elements of life. But, can you?

You Are Who You Are

You are who you are! Just as each fingerprint or DNA is unique, so too is the essence of energy that emulates from you. Though spiritual and psychological reprogramming we can each redefine ourselves and how we interact with the world. But, at the root of humanity is personality. And, from personality comes conflict. No matter how spiritual you are.

Is this good or bad? I don't know. Because as I have long detail, good or bad is simply how you define it. *"If you love Hell it becomes Heaven."*

So, what do you do when the controlling hands of other people's desire for power, greed, and domination over you extend themselves? Well, you can go and get in a fight. Somebody comes at you, and you can argue your point until you're blue in the face. Or, you can go and kick their ass. There are a lot of problems with this, however, most notably the legal consequences.

Ultimately, personal interaction is based on conflict. It is defined by who can win the battle.

How is a battle won? It is won by the person who refuses to stop until they have overpowered the other person, either by words or by fists.

This is how Cults drag people in. We all have things that we feel that are missing from our lives. That is just a by-product of human nature. The person involved in a Cult (and I use the word Cult in most wide spanning definition, including accepted religious organizations) learns to talk to a person, ask the right questions, find what the person is missing, and then promise them an antidote.

Is this right? I don't know? But, it is how religious have gained new members since the dawn of time.

But, back to the point, at this level, the individual wins the conflict by bringing another sheep into the flock. Whether are not they believe what they are preaching and promising is true or not is almost unimportant, because they have conquered another life. They have WON.

Desire

We can ultimately come to understand that all conflict is based in desire. All forms of seeking power over others are based in desire. People want to control others so they go to school; they go to the seminary, the go to the gym and learn how to fight, etc… What they are gaining at these places is a method for dominance. This is due to the fact that no matter what lie they are selling themselves, about why the doing what they are doing, studying what they are studying, they ultimately want to be MORE. MORE than other people.

The fact is, all level of individual unhappiness is based in desire. If you don't want anything else, then how can any one sway you in any direction? And, if you are content in yourself, then you have no desire to gain control or have the need to feel empowered by being MORE than any other individual.

As desire can be understood to be the controlling dominant in all those who wish to be MORE. If you simply do not play the game, then no one wins and no one losses and perfect karma is set in motion.

BE. Do what you do. Let others do what they do. And, the controlling hands of words and people who seek to be MORE will have no effect upon you.

LET GO! And, you are free.

In Your Own Moment

Since the dawning of the New Age one of the key teachings has been, that of, Getting into the Moment. Terms such as, *"Be Here Now," "Get into Your Moment,"* and *"Feel Your Now,"* have been essential components.

This ideology and these terms are meant to describe a sort of superior consciousness, where the individual is feeling some nondescript enhanced since of their life—something that the average person does not feel.

In is common that when asked, *"What does getting into the now mean?"* Or, *"What does getting into the now feel like?"* It will commonly be described by the pundits as becoming childlike, experiencing everything for the first time.

But, what does this mean? And, what are the benefits?

Somehow, in New Age spiritual circles, it has become a type of goal to revert to a childlike mind. A mind of innocence, naiveté, and trust.

From certain perspectives these may sound like ideal qualities but there is also another side to this. These are the same factors that cause the child, and the child-like, to become victims of people and society.

But, more importantly, reverting in any way, is both an impossibility and an impractical desired end-goal. The reality is, each experience we have lived, each bit of knowledge that we have taken in, has contributed to who we have become. Good or bad, all experiences have made us who we are. To some, these experiences have led to seeking out a spiritual mindset. Which has guided them to seek out the understanding of living in the now.

So, what is living in the now? And, how can this be achieved?

From a philosophic perspective, living in the now means embracing each moment as a new moment. Okay, don't we all do that anyway?

Let's think about this. How are you feeling right now? To answer for you, how you are feeling right now is how you are feeling. Thus, you are already living in your now.

Many spiritual teachers and traditions believe, however, that a person should get away from their emotions, their feelings. They should be removed from them because they are somehow based in an animalistic level of human consciousness. But, are they?

As human beings one of the essential components of our make up is emotion. Thus, emotions are a natural state. We feel! It's as simple as that.

You can try to hide from emotions. But, they will not go away.

No matter how spiritual a person claims to be, they too have emotions. As they are human, there is no way to hide themselves from emotions entirely.

This is one of the big problems when people follow teachers who are no longer alive. A dead teacher is a perfect teacher. Why? Because you will never see or experience their faults or shortcomings. All you will do is to read or hear about their superior consciousness. So, basically all you are exposed to is an enhanced description of their existence. Or, simply a lie. Because all living people have faults, just as they all have emotions.

Now, some people: the insane, the sociopathic, the selfish, the power hungry, the emotionally out of control, and the religious zealots are driven by very negative emotions that are in complete disregard to those around them. They do not care whom they harm to reach their own end-goal. But, these are not the emotions based in a normal individual.

Most of us feel happy, sad, embarrassed, frustrated, bored, in love, in anger, and all of the common emotions that are experienced throughout humanity. In terms of, *"The Now,"* these are the emotions that bring us into the now.

Think about how much of your life has passed by and you did not even notice it. Every time you ate breakfast, dinner, walked to school when you were young, drove to work, and all of the nondescript activity that make up modern life; you lived those moments, but they are gone.

Think about this, how many dinners do you remember when the food was really good (or bad), the company you were with that made you laugh and feel good (or angry), and all those times when you were really brought to an expanded emotional level. Those are the times you remember. Every time your emotions were turned-up, those are the times that truly stand out in your mind. Those are the times when you are truly in your now.

As detailed, some gurus may tell their students to rebuke emotions and live in a state of placid, meditative abyss. But, what comes from this? What comes from this is a life lived with no memories—as everything experienced is the same. Just like the boring drive to work, day after day, life all becomes a blur.

Some teachers say this non-involved emotionless mentality leads to the higher-mind. But, does it? For here is one of the ultimate illusions on the spiritual path, *"Doing nothing leads to something; enlightenment." "A silent mind is nirvana."* This is all the mumbo-jumbo of teachers who have not lived. …Teachers who have framed their teachings upon the borrowed knowledge of those who have walked the path before them. …Teachers who want to control their flock and keep them silent and mindless. Think about this, one of the key components of Zen is to become Mind-Less for only there can some level of enlightened knowledge be lived and experienced. But, all of those who teach this make excuses for themselves as to why they have not personally experienced this ultimately level of human consciousness.

It is all nonsense. It is all playing to the minds and the wallets of those on the spiritual path that seek some sort of allusive esotericism that cannot actually be had, except by the most holy. But, who is the most holy? Usually those who are dead or those whom you are not allowed to live with and see that they too actual have flaws.

Stop believing the illusion. You are living the now, right now! What you are feeling is your now. When you are hating your job, that is your now. When you are happy. When you are sad. That is your now. When you are taking your boring drive to work. That is you now. When you are making love. That is your now. When you are doing whatever it is you are doing. That is your now.

Stop trying to make, *"The Now,"* some allusive entity that you have to perform spiritual exercises to find. This is your now. What are you going to do with it?

Life is Defined by Availability

I have long discussed the fact that life is defined by availability. What this means is that your life is defined by what you have available to you. Whether this is people, money, culture, language, beauty, size, learning opportunities, friends, family, or whatever, that is what ultimate makes you who and what you are and leads to who and what you will become.

Some people are very good at pushing their opportunities of availability to the maximum limit. You see this in people who come from literally nothing and rise to the top of their profession. Many times, these are the people who are revered and even commonly referenced in the statement, *"If they can do it, so can I."* But, in reality, this is not necessarily the case. Whatever it was that gave them that ability to rise to the top was also set in motion by their set of availability. Meaning, it was a combination of their personality, desire, drive; plus who and what they knew. Plus, what they have or had is not what you have or had.

This is not to say that taking advantage of your particular set of availabilities is a bad thing. But, you cannot define yourself by what others have achieved. Moreover, you should not judge yourself or be hard on yourself due to what others have achieved and you have not—because if you are behaving in this manner, what you have set up is a mindset of self-deprecation, which only leads to a low opinion of self. From this, all kinds of negative life events are given birth to.

This being said, lack of life availability can also be seen as the one factor that holds each of us back from achieving our dreams. Lack of life availability is the ultimate demon of actualization.

This is because of the fact; we are each a creature that embraces desire. Through our culture, through the time period in which we live, and through all the desires that we are told we are supposed to have, in combination with all of those we develop, desire is the common point for all of human existence.

Our families tell us what they hope we will become. Our friends guide and share our desires as per our specific socioeconomic and cultural environment. And, we, in the quiet of our minds, focus on the dreams we hope to achieve and hold.

Now, in terms of spirituality, it is commonly taught to, *"Let go of desire."* And, this isn't a bad ideology. But, it is much harder that the words proclaim.

Desire is the defining factor of life. With this as a basis, you can either choose to live a life defined by desires—attempting to get everything that you want, which will make you live a life continually defined by gain and loss—leading to a constant state of un-peace. Or, you can choose to desire no desire. Each time a desire arises in your mind, you can beat it down. In both cases, though they arise from differing sides of the spectrum, you are defined by desire.

Life is lived by availability. You are born, you are educated, and you are surrounded by a specific culture—all framed by a specific point in history. Within that framework you are provided with a very unique and specific set of circumstances. From this, you decide which desires you allow to rise. You can decide what you want to desire. Once you have decided what you want, defined by your family, your friends, and your culture, you will then decide to either pursuit it or decided that you can never have it. So, what is ultimately the point of its pursuit? In either case, what you do next will set the next group of availabilities in motion in your life.

Most people do nothing. They do not try. They give up before they begin. Or, they try for a moment, decide it is too hard, and quit. This is not bad or good; it is simply a defining factor and a condition of the life of most people.

Others, try and try. But, the sad truth is, they try for something that is unhavebable. For example, many go after relationships with people who do not want to be in a relationship with them. An, this is just bad. It haunts both of the lives and no good ever comes from it. Ask, receive a, *"Yes,"* or a *"No,"* and move on. In other cases, people go after careers that they were just not meant to possess. Many want stardom. They want to be on the silver screen. Or, want to have their music heard across the globe. And, these are just two examples that are common here in the twenties-first century. A few generations ago, these careers would not be a source of desire at all. And, in a few generations forward, they will probably fall by the wayside. These are just a couple of examples, but they may provide you with the foundational idea of what is taking place.

But, people don't want small things. They want it, *"All."* They go to all these lengths to get that, *"All."* But, what does that, *"All,"* mean? You don't know, because you're not there. You only think that you know.

Every life situation is completely different than expected. Every life situation you live changes you forever.

Relationships go bad. Then you don't want them anymore. You're sorry you ever got involved. Jobs and careers each take their toll on your body, your mind and your spirit—no matter how seemingly great they once appeared from the distance. You never, ever know until you know…

The problem is, if you spend your life in purist, all you are left with is that pursuit. If you do not achieve it, you will be sad and unfulfilled. If you do achieve it, and it is not what you thought it was going to be, you will be sad and unfulfilled. But, the reality is, in either case, this is life, what you do is what you do. What you live is ultimately what you lived. Your life is here for only a moment. Then it is gone.

You are given a specific set of life availabilities. Maybe it is karma, a gift of god, a blessing, or a cure. But, the availabilities you are given are what you are given. Each step you take in life provides you with a new set of availabilities. Within the definition of those availabilities, you must choose who you are and what you will do with them.

You are given availabilities. Your life is lived by availability. What do you choose to do with them?

The Sanga

In the Buddhist tradition it is taught that *the Sanga* or Spiritual Community is one of the primary elements that one should take into consideration as they walk upon the Spiritual Path. To put this understanding into a more usable definition, *the Sanga* refers to the fact that, *"You can know a person by the company that they keep."* Worldly people associate with worldly people and spiritual people associate with spiritual people.

Throughout all spiritual traditions a person is told that they should let go of worldly friends and only associate with spiritually, like-minded people. On the surface, this sounds like a pretty good idea.

Think about it… For the most part a spiritually inclined person is probably not going to get you into too much trouble as they probably don't drink, do drugs, womanize (or manize), don't party, and don't do worldly activities that may have the tendency to lead you down the road to demise. Thus, you will probably remain fairly safe.

But, at this juncture, the questions must be raised, *"What exactly is spiritual?"* And, *"Who is truly a spiritual person?"*

This is the point where the novice on the Spiritual Path oftentimes becomes confused. For what appears to be spiritual is not always the truest representation of spirituality. And, those who appear to be holy are not necessarily that.

Here in the west, the obvious examples of this are the priests who mess with young children. On all levels that is just wrong. There is no excuse and no justification for that type of action.

Though these inappropriate actions have been at the forefront of the news over the past couple of decades, these actions have gone on literally forever. And, they have spanned all cultures and religious traditions.

In fact, it is so common that a person in a position of religious authority takes advantage of a person, that is it almost universally unfathomable. But, it happens everyday.

Add to this that these people are supposed representatives of God, (or whatever figure a particular religions places as its most holy). From this, these people are provided with a license to do pretty much whatever they want and claim it as an act of God. Here lies one of the primary problems with the concept of *Sanga.*

At its heart, *the Sanga* ideology if fine. But, then add to it, the desirous mind of the human personality, and the concept and all of the good it may provide is completely lost.

Watch the news when a priest or other religious figure is accused of inappropriate behavior, and you will always see people stepping up to their defense. Then, when the accusations are proven to be true, the statements arrive, *"I can't believe it. He seemed like such a good man."* And so on...

On the other side of the issue, as this type of behavior has become so prevalent, there are people who falsely claim that a person did something inappropriate to them, when, in fact, they did not. An individual does this simply to either take control over a person's life or to make that person seem less to the masses. This may be based in anger, jealously, or an untold number of other emotions. But, at the end of the day it creates the same Life-Problem attributed to that of the wayward priest; namely, the actions of another destroy and forever alter the life of a person.

Is this true spirituality?

At the heart of t*he Sanga* is people. People by their very nature, their very design, are flawed.

The human race is based upon desire. People desire THINGS. These things may be physical; they may be spiritual. But, desire is the root cause of all things both good and bad in this place we call life.

Some people desire objects. Some people desire love. Some people desire lust. Some people desire fulfillment. Some people desire enlightenment. But, no matter what the title, desire is desire.

Though it is commonly understood that a *Sanga* is made up of specified group of people who desire the same thing. But, do they?

Each person comes to the *Sanga* with their own unique set of life experiences. Each person comes to the *Sanga* with his or her own personality. Each person comes to the *Sanga* with his or her own set of desires. And though they may each be seeking a similar end-goal—though they each may desire a similar communal experience; each person is a unique and different entity. As such, they each add a particular set of variables to the overall equation.

A *Sanga* is measured by the overall output of its amassed energy. Add one faulty person to a *Sanga* and that energy is damaged and altered forever.

Each and every action we take not only affects ourselves and the overall evolution of our life, but it also affects any of those we have interaction with.

What you do today equals the choices you will be presented with tomorrow.

Who you encounter today, leads you to the people you will interact with tomorrow.

As each person is their own unique entity, you can never judge and never assume what actions they will make from moment to moment. As such, though they may present themselves as a spiritual or as a worldly person, that image they present can never truly define who they are because that is simply a projection of how they want to be viewed by the world. It is not necessarily who they truly are.

The Sanga, in its concept, is an idealize image of a perfect community and support group. Though it sounds nice, and no doubt can provide a positive learning experience, you must always keep your guard up, as you can never know what actions another person may take.

Ultimately, true spiritually is never defined by how a person appears to the world. True spiritually is only known internally. It is only defined by the True Inner Self.

Find it in you. Not outside of you.

The Yin and Yang of Insecurity

People come at life based upon one of two mindsets: confidence or insecurity. If one is confident, then they approach life with a sense of dynamic awareness. If, on the other hand, they are insecure, they come at life, and the people interactive with their life, from a space of fear, judgment, and dismissal.

As is explained in the theory of *Yin and Yang,* in all dark there is a bit of light, just as in all light there is a bit of darkness. We can also attach this understanding to the human condition of personal psychological definition and how a person behaves based upon their psychological conditioning.

There are two distinct breeds of the insecure person. The first is the meek. They are the very passive, the reserved, and the person who fades into any sphere of personal interaction they encounter because they do not feel worthy on any level of human comparison. The person who embraces this style of insecurity is commonly the one who is the most easily taken advantage of because they are easily manipulated.

The other style of insecure person is the boisterous, the outspoken, the hateful, the judgmental, and the all knowing. Though they appear to be very self-assured, in truth, they are not. In fact, they are just the opposite and that is why they behave in such a forthright manner. Thus, *Yang in the Yin.*

Due to the fact that they do not possess a clear sense of self, self-awareness, and are hiding their true inner-definition from the world, they focus on life elements outside of themselves in order to make themselves appear to be more than what they actually are or to keep the focus of other people from truly focusing on them.

Many times, the insecure person will project a position of all-knowing judgment. This, however, is just a disingenuous method to get people to not look too closely at the flaws this person possesses.

The thing about a person who bases their life upon personal insecurity is that they will rarely, if ever, state that they are an insecure person. In fact, some are so unaware of their interpersonal demons that they do not even realize it. For those who are aware of the fact that they possess an insecure mentality, many will hide this fact by any means possible in order to protect themselves from attacks and reprisals.

The number one thing that a person who is defined by insecurity will project is the mind reality of, look the other way. Do not look at me. This, as stated, may be presented by hiding from the world or it may be illustrated by throwing judgments left and right so others will think about other things and not them. In either case, the person who is based upon psychological insecurity will rarely posses the refined, discerning mindset to be able to admit their problem to themselves and dig down to the root of that life expression and thereby emerge as a whole, complete, and self-actualize individual.

The answer? There is none. As insecurity is a problem that exists within and is wholly expressed by the individual, only the individual can create a change within himself or herself. Thus, you can explain to them who they are. You can suggest what they should do and what they should stop doing. But, it is only when they choose to actually take a long hard look at themselves, study and then redefine their projection of reality that they can ever move away from being defined by insecurity.

What the Buddha Said

Historically, little is of absolute certainty regarding the life of the being who has become commonly referred to as, The Buddha. Throughout history, however, his life has been chronicled in legend.

Siddharta Guatama

Siddhartha Guatama, the Sakyamuni Buddha, *"Buddha from the Kingdom of Sakya,"* is generally agreed to have lived from 563 to 483 B.C.E. Legend states that he was a Prince who lived a very sheltered life. Upon witnessing poverty, illness, and death for the first time, he lost faith in all that was material and left behind his Royal Lifestyle, his wife, and his newborn child in pursuit of the ultimate truth of human existence.

What is historically established is that during the lifetime of The Buddha a revolution was taking place in South Asia. Iron had recently been introduced to the Indian Subcontinent from China. This led to many rapid advancements in society—agriculture was vastly improved, and landscapes could be readily cultivated. No longer were the forests the daunting obstacles they had once been. Now, they could be cleared so crops could be harvested within their once impenetrable boundaries. New structures, particularly palaces, were constructed in a much more substantial fashion. And perhaps most definitive of the era, the tool of warfare were vastly improved. So much so that near the end of his life The Buddha's own kingdom of Sakya fell to the neighboring Kingdom of Kosala. Within a century of his lifetime, the entire region of what is now Northern India and Nepal would be united as the Magadha Empire.

The prominent religion of this historic era was Vedic Brahanism. This religion can trace its roots back a thousand years prior to the life of The Buddha. Its scriptures, known as The Vedas, began to be composed in 1500 B.C.E. This religion is the basis for modern Hinduism.

The highest practitioners of this religion were the Brahmans. They were identified as the highest cast and obviously the wealthiest of this ancient society. From this, they claimed privileges not afforded to the average individual.

As formalized power, secular wealth, and religious privilege rose in this region, dissatisfaction among the populous also escalated. This gave birth to a group of ascetics who were known as Sramana. The Sramana shunned society, renounced material possessions, and became wandering holy men following an undefined path to enlightenment. This group laid the foundation for what has become more commonly known as the Sadhu. The mindset of this group, undoubtedly, influenced the path the young Siddhartha Guatama as he would ultimately follow.

The Buddha's path to enlightenment is historically unclear. It is believed that he studied with two primary teachers, Arada Kalama, who taught Akimcanya Ayatana, *"The experience of nothingness"* and, Udraka Ramaputra, who taught Naiva Samjna Asamjna Ayatana, *"The experience of conscious unconsciousness."*

The legend persists in China that Lao Tzu, the Great Sage who is credited as the author of *The Tao Te Ching,* upon becoming disheartened with Chinese society and leaving his royal post, actually entered what is modern day Nepal and also became one of

The Buddha's teachers. As romantic as the pairing of these great souls appears, there is no historic evidence to provide factual substantiation to this claim.

The Enlightenment of the Buddha

Legend states that The Buddha dissatisfied with not obtaining the ultimate understanding of life from his two teachers or following the path of a wandering holy man, sat down under a Bodhi Tree and swore he would not rise until he became enlightened. Though many legends have been written about what The Buddha experienced during this period of intensive meditation, it is known that he did, in fact, emerge an enlightened being.

The Buddha, upon his realization, gave his first enlightened discourse at what is now Bodh Gaya, near Varanasi, India. This talk is known as, *"The First Turning of the Wheel of Dharma."*

It cannot be established, with absolute certainly, what The Buddha actually said during this discourse, however. All that is written, claiming him as the source, was done so years, and in some cases centuries, after his physical death.

The Pali Canon

The Theravada tradition of Buddhism claims that the language of the Buddha was Pali, and thus, their collections of scriptures, known as, The Pali Canon, is the most accurate. This, however, has proven to be linguistically incorrect, as Pali came into existence after the time of The Buddha—who left his body near the city of Kusinagra, when he was eighty years old.

Thus, his spoken words, though possibly initially recorded in his native dialect, most probably,

Magadhi, were handed down from disciple to disciple for an undefined period before they finally found their way into scriptural form.

The Buddhist Religion

With the end of Buddha's life came the Buddhist religion. But, The Buddha did not invent the concept of enlightenment, nor was he the first or the last, being to reach this highest level of conscious evolution. Throughout the centuries, the followers of Buddhism have come to idealize his life and his teachings to the degree that it was impossible for them to reach their own Buddhahood, due to the extensive set of parameters they have assigned to the advancement of human consciousness.

There is an elemental problem with this mindset, however. Was the Buddha a Buddhist? No, he was not. He was a Hindu. Did the Buddha ask for worship? No, he did not. In fact, legend states that when he was asked, *"Are you an Avatar,"* he answered, *"No, just a man."* When asked, *"Then, are you a Guru?"* He answered, *"No, just a man."*

This is the portrait of the true, perfectly enlightened teacher, who achieved the highest level of human consciousness. Yet, he did not seek admiration due to his realization.

It is the unenlightened mind of humanity that has forgotten this simple truth and chosen to make him a deity of worship and his teachings the basis for a religion. From this mindset has come centuries of Buddhist that have been unable to encounter the realms of Nirvana—solely due to the fact that they project such an orchestrated, idealized image of what enlightenment is supposed to be. This problem is amplified by the fact that many Buddhists hold fast to the belief that the teachings of their sect of

Buddhism or their individual teachers hold the only great truth and the purest pathway to higher consciousness. They miss the point...

The teaching laid down by The Buddha are absent from formalized religion. Formalized religion employs ritual. Ritual, though beautiful to watch, is based in physical actions. Physical actions only leads to physical reactions. Thus, Karma is set in motion— not enlightenment.

If enlightenment is the core teaching of The Buddha and it is understood that it is possible for each individual to achieve this level of consciousness, then why do anything other than become enlightened? Arguing that my school or my teacher is the best and yours is wrong does not produce enlightenment. Only enlightenment produces enlightenment.

Be enlightened.

Buying Into Their Own B.S.

As I have often detailed, for whatever karmic reason, I have walked the spiritual path for most of my life. And, I use the term, *"Spiritual Path,"* for lack of a better term. But, I am referring to those of us who have decided to make the evolution of human consciousness and tuning into and understanding the great-beyond their primary focus.

As someone who has been on this road for a lot of years, I have witnessed many things about people on the path. Perhaps most disconcerting is those who buy into their own bullshit. But, I'll get into that in a moment.

People are drawn to spirituality for an untold number of reasons. Some enter the path at a young age and some much later. Most, when they decided to, *"Get Spiritual,"* find their pathway in organized religion—which is very pervasive and universally accepted in all cultures. So, it is easily at hand. Then, there are the more abstract realms of spiritually which call out to people like me. In either case, the person who has newly found the path is generally the most fervent about it.

I remember when I was a young boy of about eleven or twelve and I was sent to summer camp. One of my campmates was a young boy who used to love to make flavored toothpicks and chew on them. He brought his little bottle of liquid cinnamon spice, and he would daily dip a few toothpicks into it to keep in his mouth throughout the day. Though this seemed a bit strange and bizarre to me, what was more curious about the boy was that he had already decided what he wanted to do with his life. He was going to be a minister.

While most children of this age group have little idea of what they want to become, he had decided. Me, I wanted to grow up and be like Neil Young or Jimi Hendrix. In any case, he had set upon his path very early in life. Whether or not he ever became a minister, I don't know. But, what I do know is that youth who enter the spiritual path possess a deep belief in the possibilities of what it has to offer.

In fact, this is not only true for youth but for others who enter the path at whatever stage of their life. Once upon the path, the first step is generally to seek out a teacher to guide you down the road to your ultimate end-goal. This is where the problems begin. I have seen it so many times. A person new to the path is full of anticipation, promises, and belief. Thus, they are quick to believe whatever they hear and are easily taken advantage of.

The reality is, when a person is new to the path, they are full of exuberance. Belief equals exuberance. But, what comes next?

In this state of exuberance many desire to go out and spread this emotion to the world. They want others to be as full of joy as they are. Me too… When I was young, I wanted to tell all my friends and family about what I was experiencing and guide them to experience the same. This, even though most people do not desire to walk down this road.

As time progresses, however, and a person's knowledge becomes deeper, they generally no longer need to go out and spill their spirituality onto people who are not of the same mindset and do not desire to walk down the path. They simply become who they are and embrace their cosmic understandings in a more pure and personal space.

But then, there are the others... Those, who as they get older decided that they have something unique to give; they have found their calling. They believe that they possess something—a deeper knowledge that others do not hold. Thus, they decide to become teachers. From this, they move forward to spouting out the same recycled spiritual rhetoric that has been handed down since the dawning of advancing human consciousness. And, oh yeah, this usually equals them getting paid for what they teach or, at least, being provided with other various favors.

In formalized religious, there are generally schools that a person must attend to rise to the level of a teacher. On the spiritual path, this is generally not the case. So, anybody can go out there and claim that they have had a particular revelatory experienced and that experience is what makes them so all-knowing and the one that other people should follow. But, their experience is generally not real. It is simply something that they have read about; something that they have projected as something deep and meaningful, or simply they have realized this is a good way to attract people to follow them to feed their pocketbooks and their ego.

Mostly, what I have seen is that the people who do this, spout knowledge that they have read from books written by other people or have heard at lectures. But, whatever it is, their teachings are based upon what I call, *"Borrowed knowledge."* It does not rise from a pure, personal source—though they will, of course, argue that this is not the case till the end of their days. But, the truth is the truth.

These are the people who buy into their own bullshit. They believe they are something more than others—that they have something to offer, something to teach.

Spirituality is an organic, uniquely individual space of consciousness. Even though two people may be following the same teachings, their interpretation and internal understandings are uniquely their own. People believe they need a teacher because people seek interaction, and they seek affirmation that what they are thinking is okay. But, is what you are thinking, what you are thinking, or have you been guided to think that way?

This is the ultimate understanding of consciousness. Are you, you? Or, are you the creation of someone else's belief system?

Being you, you are free. That is nirvana. Being what someone else tells you to be is *maya*. That is illusion.

Here are a couple of simply rules so you don't step into someone else's bullshit.

Have you heard what they are saying before; from another source, perhaps said in a slightly different way?

Are they charging you for their knowledge? Knowledge is free. It doesn't cost a dime.

Are they calling you, *"My child, my loved-one, my dear-one?"* If they are, they are projecting that they are more than you. No one is more than you. You are the source of your own spirituality and enlightenment. Be you. Not a student of someone who buys into their own bullshit.

Are You Controlling Your Anger or is Your Anger Controlling You?

In our lives it is inevitable that each of us will encounter situations that we are not happy with. These situations can be defined by all kinds of variables but at the root of all of them is the fact that their occurrence makes us unhappy.

The question must be asked, *"Where does our unhappiness arise from?"* The answer to that question is quite simple—where dissatisfaction arises from is our desire for a particular life-situation to be played out in a certain manner of our choosing, but it is not.

Many people, when encountering a life situation that makes them unhappy, observe it for what it is. Yes, they may be become unhappy, frustrated, depressed, or even angry but they do not express these emotions in an unsavory manner. They may tell the person who is causing the situation that they are unhappy or even angry with what they are doing but they are mature enough to know that most life situations are not so important to allow the emotions that they evoke to move forward from that moment and define an entire life. Meaning, any actions you take when you are dissatisfied or angry should not be so all-encompassing that they may come to defining the rest of your existence or negatively influence the existence of any other person.

The truth be told, the majority of this world's population is very selfish. People are out for themselves—they only think about themselves or those they care about, and the rest of the world be damned. For those of us who walk the path of consciousness we may believe that this is the wrong way to encounter the world. None-the-less, this is the way it is. And, though we may hope to raise the overall consciousness of the world by us being the best person we can be, the majority of humanity does not possess this mindset. So, what are we left with? We are left with a world defined by individual desire and people acting out whenever their personal desires are not being met.

How do you act when you are not happy? How do you act when you are not getting what you want? How do you behave when you are angry? The answer to these questions is not only what sets the course for your own existence into motion but it also, at least partially, defines the lives of all those people who interact with you. And, from there, it moves outwards to all of those people who interact with those people you have interacted with.

Here is a fact, few people ever take into consideration how what they are doing and how they are behaving is affecting their own evolution let-alone the lives of others whenever they are acting-out in an unenlightened manner.

How you behave in any given moment, how you react to your desires either being met or not being met, projects from you out onto the entire world. If, when are angry, you study this emotion and come to a deeper understanding of SELF, the world becomes a better place. This is because of the fact that you, personally, have become a more aware individual. If, on the other hand, you explode with your uncontrolled anger whenever you are not happy with the cards life has dealt you, this means that not only have you affected your own inner evolution in a negative manner but you have also negatively affect the lives of all those around you by not controlling your angry outbursts and irrational behavior. From this, not only have you personally become defined by your explosive nature, but you make the lives of all of those people around you, whom you have forced to become aware of and interactive with your anger, much worse.

If you want to keep YOU as the central focus of all your thoughts and actions understand this, if you have hurt anyone by your actions or your behavior, no matter whether consciously or unconsciously, you have hurt yourself. That is what karma is.

Ultimately, you are the source point of the rest of the world! If you understand this, then you become much more thoughtful about allowing your emotion to be in control of you as opposed to you being in control of them.

Again, it must be stated, most people don't care. They do what they do with complete disregard for others. They feel they are justified in their emotions, deeds, and actions. If confronted with the fact of what they have done or how they have behaved is negatively affect the lives of others, at best, they will simply make excuses for their actions and/or claim they have the right to feel the way they want to feel—to behave the way they want to behave. They may even attempt to turn the scenario around on the individual who is expressing to them how their negative emotional actions are hurtful to the lives of others. But, all this is based upon are the excuses of an unenlightened individual who has allowed their emotions to run ramped and come to control them.

This is the source point for the dilemma of human emotion. People are emotional creatures. People find justification for their actions. People try to blame others, god, and life, for the way they are feeling. If a person has become entrenched in negative emotional behavior and/or negative emotional outbursts, they find some-one or some-philosophy to give them a logical and justifiable justification for the way they are behaving. What they do not do, however, is looking deeply within themselves, see that they are living their life in a negative manner, and thereby come to fix their internal psychological apparatus.

So, what can you, (as the person who chooses to live a life of positive consciousness), do? First of all, if you are one of those people who is defined by frustration and anger, take a long hard look at your life. Find out what you are dissatisfied or angry about. Most probably you will come to the conclusion that it is based upon you not getting the things you want, being with the people you want, achieving the goals you have set for yourself, or living the life and the lifestyle you had envisioned for yourself. Okay, so now you know. Now what? Here is the thing, you can work towards your dreams, but if working towards your dreams is based upon a mindset of anger, your dreams will be defined by anger-filled accomplished if they are ever lived at all. If you based your life upon constantly embracing the negative emotions of frustration and anger, all you will encounter is defeat—which will probably lead you to more anger. Why? Because not only have you locked yourself into constantly embracing a negative and self-defeating emotion but due to this emotion you have negatively affect the lives of all those you have encounter. Yes, you can lie to them and pretend to be something you are not. But, at the root of all personal growth and self-actualization is to embrace who you truly are, refine that inner being as necessary, and then project that positivity to the world. If you are good, you will be seen as good. If you have helped people and not hurt people, those who can help you will be more willing to do so. But, if you hurt yourself and hurt other through your unrelenting anger and frustration, what image and what energy do you think you are projecting to the world?

Negative only equals negativity. If you focus your life based upon negative emotions, you project those emotions from your inner being onto all those you interact with. No lie will hide the truth and only negativity can be born from negativity.

Life begins and ends with you. This is YOUR life. How are you going to live it? Is it going to be defined by your anger and your frustrations—letting those negative emotions emulate from you and define all of your personal life-space and relationships? Or, are you going to become MORE, are you going to delve into the essence of your being, analyzing and overcoming all negativity, fix any negativity you have unleashed, and not let something so temporary as an emotion come to define the definition of you to the world?

Can I Be More?

At the heart of all advancing human consciousness is the desire for the individual, (for you), to become more. Advancing human consciousness is set in motion by the individual. Though random things happen throughout all of our lives that make us think and rethink our existence and how we interact with life, it is only when we consciously choose to change, choose to become better, choose to become mentally and spiritually more, that we actually move our personal understanding of human consciousness to a higher realm of spiritual insight.

It is essential to note that the of fact of life is, most people do not care about progressing their understanding of consciousness. This is commonly the case if an individual is content with where they are in their life. For example, they might state, I am going to school, I have a good job, a good girlfriend or boyfriend, wife or husband, I love my kids, I live in a nice house, and so on. As they are content and their basic needs are being met, why should they ponder their inner-workings and attempted to become a more complete individual?

The other side of the issue and another reason why many people never attempt to consciously alter their life course is that they are angry at the world. I hate my life! I had a horrible childhood, I have a crappy job, my life is not turning out the way I thought it would, everybody has more money and they live a better life than me, my wife left me and took all my money, I caught my husband cheating, I got caught and arrested for committing that crime, I can't find a girlfriend or a boyfriend, and the list goes on but you get the point. Here, in this state of mind, the individual is too internally angry at their own life to have the wherewithal to step outside of themselves long enough to actually take a long hard look at where they are in life, why they are there, and then consciously decide what they can do about it.

There is one final category of a person who does not care to refocus their life and climb the ladder of rising consciousness. That is the person who is lost someone in the middle of the two previous extremes. Their life is okay; not bad, not good, but not so horrible that they are forced to make a change. Thus, they progress through their existence and just do the chores of day-to-day life with little or no thought.

Here, it must be stated that none of the previously mentioned categories of individual existence are bad in and of themselves. They are simply examples of the way many people interact with life. But, what is born from existing on this level of unrefined human consciousness is that negativity spreads from the individual onto the rest of the world causing ongoing chaos, unhappiness, anger, and destruction. For, from an unfocused, uncaring mindset, people do bad things to other people, other life creatures, to the world, and the universe on the whole. As they are only focused and thinking about themselves, they do not care and are, in fact, commonly completely unaware of any damage they instigate.

As I often speak about, your words—what you say about yourself and what you say about other people does more to describe your inner being and your interpersonal thought process than virtually anything else. What do you say about yourself? Is it braggadocios or it is humble? What do you say about other people? Is it positive or is it negative? If it is positive, then positive emotions and reactions are set into motion. If it is negative, then further negative emotions and reactions are set into motion. Thus, what you say sets an entire course of world-reactions into motion.

Some people gain power in this. They somehow feel that by spewing out all kinds of judgmental negativity that they are shaping the minds of others about whatever they are speaking about. For a specific moment, at a specific point in time, that may be true, and it may make them feel empowered. But, all negativity does is to set further life-negativity into motion. This is why those who exist on this plane of consciousness are the first to balk once negativity is focused on them which will inevitability happen as whatever you choose to release from yourself travels to the world around you and attracts the type and the style of person that is draw to those who propagate that level of energy.

This is the same with those who are focused upon presenting positive thoughts, ideas, and actions. From them arise a calming and directed energy that is allowed to spread out and beyond themselves. As such, those who seek these positive thoughts are drawing to them, making their life ultimately better as they are presenting a nurturing force to all those they encounter.

Life, and the choice to be more, happens internally. Though it may be projected from the inside out, where it takes shape and form, it arises from within the individual, (within you).

Many people claim to be something they are not. Many people project a specific mind-ideology to the people they meet but it is false. The problem with people who live on this plane of existence is that by the time a person has gotten to know them well enough to realize that they are a fake, that they are not truly who they claim to be, time and life-experience has gone by. As a person was lured into a relationship with a specific individual by the person being wily enough to be able to preset a false persona, then so much negativity has been set into motion by their deceit that it may never be overcome. It is for this reason that whenever you meet a person who makes claims about being a This or a That listen closely to their words, look at where their life is, how they are living—for where they are in life in terms of their age and their means can truly detail if a person is who they claim to be.

Look, See, Listen, Know.

134

Here lies the introductory step for those who desire to become more and raise their consciousness to a level where (you) personally become a better person and you aid in the evolution of world consciousness. First, you must decide that you want to leave behind the trappings of all the things that held you back from being a person who desires to focus their life on raising human consciousness. You must choose to become better and become more. Then, you must forgo any ego that comes with this mindset. Never claim, *"I am."* Simply be, then you are. Next, shed all of those in your life who hold you to any negative thought process that you no longer wish to possess and truly peer into those who claim to speak of positivity before you allow them into your life. Finally, choose to be your own barometer, choose to be your own judge and jury. Consciously see who you are and then take note of what you are thinking, what you are saying, how you are behaving, and what impact what you do has on those, (and the world), around you. If you are thinking good thoughts, saying good words, doing good things, focusing your mind on betterment, not negativity, then you will begin to observe the results of rising human consciousness.

Ultimately, deciding to become more is not an ego-based exercise. It is you understanding that there is a better state of life-consciousness, a better way of life-interaction, and then you begin to strip away the negative layers of yourself revealing a better you which makes all people you interact with better and this whole world-place just a little bit more peaceful.

Defined by Others

In each of our lives we are in a constant pattern of human interaction. Whether we work in a large facility with hundreds of people or we simply walk down the street, there are people everywhere. …Whether we must formally communicate with people one-on-one or we are locked in a basement staring at the world through a television or the internet, people are all around us. Some of these people we know. Some of these people we know about. Some of these people we have no idea that they even exist, but they are there.

In life, as we are forced into human interaction, we must decide how that interaction will take place. Some people are nice—they are self-fulfilled, conscious of their place in this world, and try to make everyone's life just a little bit better. Others are self-involved, self-loathing, power-trippers, dominate, and/or unthinking. Most people fall somewhere in between of these two extremes. This is the world. These are the people that inhabit it.

As we pass through life other people come to define who we are. In some cases, this is by choice. We like how a person looks, what they say, what they do, and we attempt to follow a similar path as what they are living. In other cases, people force their way into our life through anger, violence, or uncaring/unthinking behavior. This is simply the condition of life. These are the people that are here.

The question then arises, if you are a conscious person, walking the path to self-actualization, how do you let other people define who you are? They are out there. You are here. You will be forced to interact with them. What are going to do?

Many people, when they encounter a strong person, an individual with an overwhelming presence, melt once they are in their company. Others, immediately attempt to out-presence them. From this, conflict is given birth to.

Many people when they encounter a passive person, an individual unsure of themselves and non-outgoing, attempt to take advantage of them. Others attempt to guide them to a higher state of self, where they will not be overtaken by the powerful and the dynamic. This is where the student/teacher relationship is given birth to. …But, the teacher is always in the position of authority, however. What is the personal motivation for a person who seeks to become a teacher?

Though the previously discussed examples are made up of the more extreme illustrations of human interaction, who we interact with and how we allow them to define us also taken place on the interpersonal level. What are you thinking about? Is it a person? Why are you thinking about them? Why are you obsessing about them? What do you hope to gain by thinking about them?

In life, how we allow people to define us is more on the level of the mind than it is on the level of the physical. In fact, physical interaction are much more definable. …A person did this. A person said that. From what they did or said we react and from that we can reach an understandable conclusion. On the mind level, however, this becomes much more convoluted as it is only in the personal mind. Therefore, it is only defined by the individual's mind. And, each person's mind is formed and defined by an untold number of irrational, unreasonable thoughts. But, as the thoughts, desires, and ideologies are locked into the mind, no one else can peer into them. The mind, and this individualized mindset, is where all of the damnation and the bad deeds done to the world are nourished and harvested. How much are you locked into your mind?

When we live a physical existence, when we are forced to interact and communicate with people on a frequent basis, person-to-person, and not by some less than personal method like on the telephone, internet, or smartphone, we are forced to live the life of the world, in the world. From this, there is little time to find the need to obsess about the meaningless nothings that can come to haunt the individual mind. On the other hand, when a person is left alone much of the time, all they have to do is find a thing or, more than likely, a person to obsess about. From this, be it bad or good, that person comes to define their life.

Why do you want anyone, any other person, to define your life? Why do you want to be like any other person? Why do you want to think about what another person has done or said? Why do you want to do or say what another person has done or said? Why do you want to hold on to personal interactions longer than when they took place? Why do you want to think, obsess, stalk, or imitate another person? Why can't you be yourself?

In life, we each learn from other people. That is a fact. If we are a conscious individual, we may learn what not to do by watching what they have done. In life, we may see or hear an individual's negative behavior and what occurs from it and then we may choose to never act or behave in that manner. Also, in life we may observe the reaction when someone does something selfless and giving — expecting nothing in return. From this, we may decide to stop thinking only about ourselves and how we are feeling, in any given moment, and we may enter into a pathway of giving and caring first. Yes, we may have learned this from observing another person—come to understand what is the best way to behave but from there it is we who must make this behavior our own.

Let go of the thinking about others. Thereby, you no longer allow them to define you. Become the most perfect example of YOU and whom you should be.

Be yourself. Don't be defined by others.

Do You Listen to Yourself?

Most people spend their entire life talking. They listen but they only listen to others. They never listen to themselves. They talk and they talk, they listen and they listen but they never hear.

Do you ever think about what you are saying? Do you think about what you say before you say it? Do you contemplate the effect your words have on other people? Do you ever think about what you say and how it sounds to other people? Do you ever question why you say the things you say?

At the root of higher consciousness is the individual who can step away from themselves. At the root of higher consciousness is the person who can be silent instead of attempting to make themselves heard. At the root of higher consciousness is the person who surrenders their ego and does not have to win the discussion. At the root of higher consciousness is the person who is whole onto themselves and thereby knows why they speak the words they speak.

In this world we have been taught to speak up, speak out, say what is on our mind. In this world we have been taught to fight for what we believe in. But, why do we believe in anything? Ask yourself, why do you believe what you believe? Why do you feel you have to voice what you believe? Who gives you the right to say anything?

Each of us possesses a personality. Each of us holds onto all the factors that have educated us throughout our life. Each of us believes that because we are, we are. But, are we?

Who are you? Why are You? Who gave you permission to be you? And, why do you feel you have the right to spread your you onto others?

There is one factor that dominates all conversations and that is personal ego. You feel you know enough to tell others how they should be, what they should be, and how they should feel. But, if you believe this that means that you are ego dominated and not a truly whole and pure person. For the true knower understands and acknowledges that they know nothing; no one does.

If you speak, it is your ego that is speaking. If you talk, it is your self-absorption that is talking. It is your belief in yourself. But, step back and truly take a look at who and what you are. Are you the truth in your words or are you simply trying to make yourself be seen as something more in the eyes of other people? If you are talking, then that means that the ladder is the case. You are just spewing ego trying to make yourself believe that you are more and make others believes that you hold the answers. But, more is never the goal of the enlightened mind. Less is more. That is why those who hold true knowledge never speak. They never try to tell people anything. They never attempt to convince people of how they should think or what they should believe. Mostly, they never lie.

If you lie, all you are is a liar. It is as simple as that. Knowing that fact alone should cause you to be silent.

Next time you are speaking to someone have the mental aptitude to step back from yourself and listen to how you sound. Become aware of how others perceive how you speak. Put away your ego and listen. Once you do that you will most likely become silent.

I was in a shop today, kneeling down looking at something on the bottom shelf. A woman, pushing her shopping cart, drives it straight into my ankle. She hit me right in that spot that really hurts when your ankle is impacted. I jump up, *"Ouch, Damn it!"* The woman seemed completely oblivious to what she had done. Or, maybe she just didn't care? I looked at her. Finally, she inquires, *"What happened?" "You just hit me in the ankle with your shopping cart!"* But, that was it. She didn't acknowledge what she had done. She didn't say, *"I'm sorry,"* like most of us would have said. She didn't ask if she could help. She just stood there ignoring me and studying what she was considering buying. Now, with my ankle hurting I became very disinterested in buying anything, I state, *"Why don't you open your eyes,"* and I walked away.

Behavior like this, on the part of that woman, is very revealing about life and human interaction. Some people are very caring and conscious about how the impact and interact with the world. Others are not. Certainly, at times, we are each distracted and do something that we didn't mean to do. But, for most of us, those incidences are few and far between. There are other people, however, who perform unconscious actions all the time and simply give it no thought.

People like this may or may not know that they are doing things that impact and/or injure the life of others. Some know and do it anyway. That is simply wrong. Others are so unconscious of their place in life that they do things and are not even aware of them. At best, when confront with this fact, they make excuses or lie. Then, there are those, who like this lady, do something and for whatever reason refuse to take any responsibility for it.

If you live your life in this fashion, you are truly

141

living at the lowest level of human consciousness. For any of us to be better and more whole, we must first become a witness to our life and then strive to become the best that we can be. This includes observing and acknowledging all of our actions, be they good or bad.

Now, one could speculate why a person behaves in this non-remorseful manner. But, at best, that would be guesswork. Each person has their own life motivations and though we can chart and study them it is only that individual person who is ultimately in control of how they behave as they interact with this world.

Most definitely, the majority of us would cast the blame on the person who performs a negative action. But, if they are too locked into their own mind, not caring what they do and/or whom they harm, why would this even matter to them? They don't care what we think, and they don't care who they hurt.

One of the great things about long-term training in the martial arts is that it teaches a person to become very aware, even hyperaware, of their environment. As they are constantly schooling their body and their mind to anticipate the next move of their opponent, they become extremely mindful of all that is taking place around themselves. From this, they gain a very profound enhanced perception of the world.

This too is the case with meditation. You can always tell someone who meditates. They are calm, focused, and very aware. They are not lost in an over exaggerated sense of self, thus they are not dominated by anger, greed, lust, desire, and the need to perform hurtful actions whether consciously or not.

Just as you can easily distinguish someone who meditates, you can also recognize someone who does not. People like this are out of control of their emotions, they are ego driven, they think only about themselves, they lie to achieve their desired ends, and they unleash unconscious actions; just like this lady did to me, with no sense of remorse.

Your life is defined by your focus. If you live in a space dominated by desires, denial, and emotions—not caring about whom you harm, then what will be the ultimate outcome of your life? What will happen is that you will pass through life constantly defined by your happiness or your sadness, your anger, or your exuberance. You will never know peace, as you will not be defined by understanding the greater good. Furthermore, as you are not going out of your way to put your own desires on hold: to elevate the great whole, to do conscious and positive things for other people and this world, then your life will pass by defined only by your selfish, negative, and controversial actions and interactions.

Caring only about yourself is caring only about yourself. That is a very hollow place to base your life upon.

Ask yourself, *"Why are you doing what you are doing?"* Look deep for this answer, don't just pass over it with, *"Because it makes me feel good,"* or something like that. Look deep. Why do you do what you do? Why do you behave the way you behave? How do you interact with other people? Do you care about them? Or, do you only care about yourself and are only interactively nice and responsible when it adds to what you believe is your betterment?

It is very important to step beyond yourself in life. It is very important to stop casting your individualized definitions onto other people. It is very important to care about other people and do good things for them. Most importantly, it is essential to live your life from a place of consciousness; taking others into consideration before you built up a wall around yourself believing that you are the only one that matters, because you are not.

Choose to give before you take. Choose to know yourself and do good things. Choose to never hurt anyone for any reason. Choose to fix what you have broken.

Karma

Before I get into the whole who, what, when, where, and why of Karma, I believe that it is important to discuss one of the most essential issue of Karma—why people turn to this understanding for answers.

People commonly ask, *"Why has somebody else achieved something?"* *"Why have they, when I have not?"*

If you wonder why, you have not achieved your life goals and desires, the first place you need to look is yourself.

Do you live your life from a place of positivity and goodness, or do you live your life based in negativity?

Negativity is expressed in many ways: anger, criticism, violence, dishonesty, and so on. If you perform these actions, then you have developed bad Karma. It is as simply as that.

If you live your life embracing negativity, that is the answer to the questions of why you have not achieved your life goals. For if you live your life at this level, negativity attracts negativity, and you will never be able to live your dreams—because negativity is against the greater good of mankind and the universe.

If you find that you have been living your life embracing negativity, and you want to change, the question may then be asked, *"What can I do to change?"* Well, the first thing you must do is you must stop performing negative actions. Then, you must repair the negativity you have unleashed.

What does this mean? You must replace your negativity with positivity.

First of all, do not attempt to justify your actions by stating, *"I didn't like that person or that person deserved it."*

Who are you to judge!

As long as you negatively judge others, it is you who will inhibit your own growth as a conscious individual.

Or, *"I did it because of my negative cultural programing, my bad childhood, or my family genetics."*

Stop that! Take responsibility for your actions!

Furthermore, repairing your karma is not like going to confession and being told to recite one hundred *"Our Fathers,"* or one hundred *"Hail Mary's."* Those actions may right you with your priest, but it does not right you with the person or person's you have unleashed negativity against.

It is kind of like saying, *"I'm sorry."* That statement means nothing, if you do not do something to truly prove that you are sorry.

What you must do is, you must right your wrongs!

How is this achieved? That depends on what you have done.

If you have stolen, you must repay those who you have stolen from. If you have lied, you must tell the truth. If you have criticized, you must replace that criticism with praise. If you have injured, you must repair the damage.

Many people wonder why Karma hits them so hard. This is because they do not set about on a path of positivity and consciously attempt to right the wrongs they have committed.

Repair your own Karma.

Try it and you will be amazed at the results. Positivity will enter your life and you will much more readily achieve your goals.

It is you who must do this. No one can do it for you. Right your wrongs!

Now that I detailed the secret to repairing Bad Karma, we can continue forward and investigate the foundations of this ancient understanding.

The Foundations of Karma

The Sanskrit word Karma, literally translated, means *"Action."* This word represents the law of cause and effect, *"As yee sew, so shall yee reap."*

Karma Yoga is the Yoga of Self-Transcending Action.

Karma

Karma is one of the most complicated and profoundly philosophical issues you must deal with on your path towards spiritual realization. Because of the fact, right and wrong, good or bad are not universally defined in this physical world. Not only does each culture possesses a somewhat differing view of right and wrong but each person holds their own values and individual perceptions of good and bad. Certainly, there are distinct wrongs: hurting someone unnecessarily, forcefully taking something from another person, being selfish and uncaring, and so on. But beyond these obvious instances, the precise definition becomes lost. For example, what about when you hurt someone unintentionally? Or, while pursuing the Spiritual Path, you must leave someone behind, thus, causing him or her to suffer at your absence?

The question of Karma is amplified when people justify the wrongs they are performing for what they believe to be a just cause. For example, how many people have died in wars on this Earth motivated by religious idealism?

Perhaps even more disconcerting is the case of individuals who continually cause physical and emotional pain to other people. Yet somehow, their life seems to continue forward in an unhindered path of success and acquisition. When justifying their negative Karmic actions, these people oftentimes allude to the fact that they had a bad childhood, are getting back at the world for what was done to them, or due to negative peer influence they were guided down the wrong road. Though these may be psychologically valid rationalizations, none-the-less, negative actions have taken place, often times injuring good people.

On the other side of the coin, there are those individuals who continually provide a positive service to the world. Yet, they are confounded by continued negative encounters. Why should adverse experiences happen to these people if they are expounding good to humanity?

The philosophic debate on the nuances of Karma has gone on for centuries. And, it will continue. In ancient Vedic texts, three levels of Karma are defined which may provide you with some insight into the various types of Karmic action which are taking place in this material world.

The Three Levels of Karma

The three levels of Karma are: Sanchita Karma, *"Accumulated Karma,"* Prarabdha Karma, *"Actions which create Karma: good or bad,"* and Kriyamana Karma, *"Current actions."*

1. Sanchita or Accumulated Karma is the Karma that you have previously substantiated. Sanchita Karma, not only defines actions that you have taken in this life, but also actions that you performed in previous incarnations. Many believe that this is one of the primary components that go into the formation of an individual's personality—as they are acting out a life style and mindset which they substantiated in a previous life.

The understanding of Sanchita Karma is also used to define why seemingly good people, in their present incarnation, encounter negative events in their life. It is understood that though they may now be very good, in a previous existence, they must have created adverse Karma. Thus, they suffer in this lifetime.

Certainly, in the Western world, the concept of paying for sins from a previous life strikes an adverse chord in many people. This is because of the fact that they believe that their current body is their only body and even if they do accept the theory of reincarnation, why should they have to pay the price for an existence that they no longer have any control over? This is where the belief systems indoctrinated by religion comes into play in the definition of Karma. For example, a Hindu or a Buddhist would simply let go of philosophic questioning and relinquish themselves to accepting the understanding of Sanchita Karma as fact. Thus, any life occurrence, be it positive or negative, is quickly rationalized and accepted as Karma.

2. Prarabdha Karma is the Karma that has come into existence due to past actions. Illustrative of this type of Karma is the individual who performs negative acts, for what ever physical, emotional, or

psychological rational, and then later in their life they encounter unfavorable situations. These events may take place in the next life, the distant future or may happen almost instantaneously. This understanding provides some solace to people who have been wronged by others—as they know, sooner or later, that unjust individual will have to pay the price for their actions.

It is additionally understood at this level of Karmic understanding, if one's Karmic debt is paid up, then any Karmic retribution for a negative act will be incurred relatively quickly, as there is not a long backlog of wrongs waiting to be repaid.

Prarabdha Karma not only details the events that occur as a result of adverse Karma, but it is also equally applicable to positive Karma, as well. This can explain why the rare case of a truly negative person, in this life, continually encounters seemingly positive experiences—they were a very good person in a past life.

3. Kriyamana Karma is the actions you take which lay the foundation for either positive or negative Karma in the future.

Some people were born into economically poor living conditions, dysfunctional families, or have had childhoods corrupted by very bad influences and occurrences. Others have experienced a relatively positive childhood only to be impacted by negative influences, as they have grown older. Sociologists and Psychologists have, for decades, attempted to draw conclusions to why an individual follows a particular path in life, due to foundational attributes. Though there is, no doubt, quantitative validity to some of their findings, it must be ultimately understood that we each are the masters of our own destiny. At any point in life, be it before you instigated any adverse Karma or post having unleashed a plethora of negativity, you can take back your life and choose to consciously move forward—doing good things for the world, creating good Karma, even while you suffer the inevitable repercussions for actions you have taken in the past.

Certainly, most of us have encountered influences in our lives that were not of the purest content. Additionally, due to innumerable psychological factors we have walked down impure paths with people we should not have. Under these influences most of us have all performed acts that we now can see as, *"Bad Karma."* Knowing this, you have two options in your life. One, you can hold on to those experiences and allow them to set a pattern for the rest of your life. Two, you can consciously let go of the past and move forward into a world where you will never allow negative people or situations to guide you again. With this more positive approach, you allow yourself to live each new moment of life in a positive fashion—following the path to Self Realization while you do good things for all those you encounter.

Creators of Karma

From ancient Vedic texts we learn that once one's personality is initially set in motion by Sanchita Karma, the individual then moves forward into life choosing to act out one of three levels of Karma: Sattva, Rajas, or Tamasa. These three types of Karma parallel the understanding, known in Sanskrit as Gunas, or *"The Three States of Consciousness."*

Sattva is the pure state. Rajas, is the active, passionate state. Tamas, is the dark, overripe state.

The Sanskrit word Karman is used to describe an individual who is creating a specific type of Karma. Thus, an individual is either a Sattva Karman, Rajas Karman, or a Tamas Karman.

The Sattva Karman's actions are pure, precise, and directed towards a higher good each step of the way. A Rajas Karman's actions are all performed from a sense of ego—everything is done for the betterment of himself. A Tamas Karman's actions are performed from a dark, deluded, and confused state of mind. Serving no one and nothing.

Karma and the Human Being

Existing in a human body means that everyone, no matter how holy, is bound by Karma. It must be ultimately understood that no act is wholly good and bad. What may benefit one may cause pain to another. Thus, as we are bound by the complexities of human existence, good and bad will remain an individual's perception.

The Yogi does all that he can to create a positive world: forgiving those who have hurt him, helping those who need help, guiding those who need guidance. Any action is attempted from only the most pure of motivations, understanding that, ultimately; each person is their own person, with their own emotions, desires—cultural and psychological influences. You cannot make everyone happy. Thus, the Yogi walks his path, embracing life and attempting to do the most possible good each step of the way.

Karma Yoga

Karma Yoga is the *"Yoga of Self Transcending Action."* What this means is that the individual puts his own desires aside and performs acts for the betterment of God, society, a specific group, a particular person, or the world as a whole.

The purpose of Karma Yoga is two-fold: first of all it is a meditation in selflessness. It teaches the practitioner that there is a higher good and due to the fact that we are in the material world, physical actions must be taken to achieve this wide spanning righteousness. Secondarily, Karma Yoga, instructs the devotee to make all physical actions a conscious gift to God. Thus, everything one does is an act of reverence.

Karma Yoga witnesses the practitioner doing acts, without any debate, which are oftentimes actions which one would normally not undertake. We as human beings each have our own predetermined sets of parameters that we believe is our station in life. These have been instigated from a combination of factors: our upbringing, our financial condition, and our self-image, to name only a few. What these predetermined set of parameters does is to cause us to take action which are deemed normal and appropriate to us. Though these actions may lead to the betterment of our personal lives, they, oftentimes, do nothing for another person or the advancement of the world as a whole.

The Karma Yogi steps beyond the boundaries of the accepted norm and performs whatever actions are necessary to help another individual or cause— even if these actions are a large step downwards from one's position in life. This is why Karma Yoga is considered an act of selflessness. As one is performing these acts, the mindset of, *"This is below me,"* or *"I am better than this,"* is never contemplated. Instead, the act itself is seen as cultivating necessary humility in the individual and the person performs it to perfection, only wishing to provide a helping service.

Many times, a Karma Yogi is given specific actions to perform by his Guru. As the spiritual teacher is understood to be all knowing, it is immediately understood that these actions are a necessary action in the Karmic unfoldment of the individual. Thus, they are immediately performed.

As a meditation device Karma Yoga is a great tool as it causes the Yogi to raise his mind above the limited perceptions of the self and move towards a mindset where all people are interactive parts of the cosmic whole—none, more or less than another. This is why a Karma Yogi often times performs no formal seated meditation. Instead, they focus all of their Sadhana upon the positive actions they are performing in the name of Karma Yoga.

On a much deeper level, the Karma Yogi performs all actions as reverence to God. The Karma Yogi does nothing that will knowingly injure another person or damage any aspect of this world. All they do, they do in the name of God. They see God in every aspect of humanity, nature, and even material objects of this physical plane. Thus, every action is taken with the embracing of the knowledge that God is being served.

Misinterpreted Karma Yoga

There are those who believe that by performing actions in service of another person they will automatically be repaid with, *"Good Karma."* This mindset is completely false. The Karma Yogi seeks no repayment. All actions are simply taken as a gift to the universal good. If positive reaction comes from this—that is fine, but it is never sought after.

Some very pure spirited people truly obtain joy from helping the less fortunate and providing service or giving money to others. Though these are good and helpful actions, they are not necessarily Karma Yoga. For if one performs any actions with the slightest glimmer of ego gratification, self worth, or superiority then the action is lost from being truly holy.

Karma Yoga is not about obtaining joy or satisfaction from your works, nor is it about the varying degrees of egotism that may arise from helping those you see as having less than yourself. Karma Yoga is a meditative pathway of complete self-abandonment, letting go of all of your thoughts, and emotions, while performing service for the betterment of humanity, while devoting your actions to God.

A Karma Yogi strives to be selfless in every movement in life. What he does, he does—he seeks no thanks or congratulations. He understands that every action is a combination of good and bad. No movement in this physical world is wholly free from possible negative ramifications. Thus, he does all he can to serve others and provide a positive service to the world, hoping to limit evil and bring about everlasting good.

I frequently warn people about the fact that there are many people out there who learn the words and the actions of a certain form of spirituality and then they go out and market it to the masses. There are certainly those who, from start to finish, do this as a means to make money and/or gain power over others. But, the fact of the matter is, there are far more who enter this roadway to disaster by first desiring to become something spiritual themselves. It is somewhere after this point, however, that it all goes awry.

For someone to embrace any level of higher consciousness on the pathway to spirituality they must first believe that there is something more; something greater than ourselves out there. This is where all of the folly begins. For as long as you hope for, desire, want to believe that you are not whole onto yourself there is the temptation to look outside of yourself for answers. Certainly, religion has played upon this forever. And, from the boundaries of religion many a person has come to the pulpit claiming religion as their basis and then moved from the true realms of spirituality onto become nothing more than a desirous self-serving individual. We have all heard the stories…

The fact is, throughout all societies on this planet, throughout all periods of history, there has existed the promise of religion and spirituality. *"If you do this, you will get that. Be good and you will go to heaven. Be bad and you will go to hell. If you are not getting what you want out of life it is because you are not spiritual or pure enough. It is your fault! Or, god is testing you. But, I can guide you to the realm where you can be better, purer, more holy and from my guidance you will receive what you truly desire."*

This is where the con begins. This is where the con has always begun. It is never based upon spirituality; it is based upon the ego of the teacher. The internal belief that, *"I have something to give you."* From this there has been born the ruination of the lives of so many believers. ...Believers that were hoping for the path to the truth, to God Consciousness, to a better life. Yet, all they received was the false guidance of a false teacher.

People who teach, people who claim to be spiritual or know anything spiritual must first learn the rules of spirituality. They must study what has already been said so they will fit into the mindset that is understood to be spirituality within any specific mindset, in a specific region or time in this life-space. A person needs to know what is believed. They must study what is believed. Then, once they have, they have the ability to go out to the masses and tell them what they want to hear.

In times gone past, very specific elements or very specific religions were all that inhabited a very specific placement of this earth's geography. What was believed here, was not believed there. As time and the physical movement of humanity expanded across the globe so too did the concept of, *"What I believe it right, what you believe is wrong."* From this was born wars and all types of treachery. As the religious wars subsided, the various beliefs of the various religions and philosophic cultures came to be intermingled. From this, a mess of varying philosophic ideology was given birth to and accepted. One could mix this religion with that philosophy and call it something whole and organic onto itself. But, was it? No, it was simply a mixture of Mind Junk that someone conjured up and called it something. This trend has moved on-and-on throughout the world cultures giving birth to many a person who claimed to be a knower of something. The problem is, no longer do they have to be a true anything—a certified teacher. All that have to be is a person who has mastered the rhetoric. Just as religious wars destroyed many a person's life; from the past up to this modern day, so too have the false prophets ruined many a person's life.

Hand-in-hand with this modern-day rhetoric-tactician, and the intermixing of religious philosophies came the way out. The method to not take responsibly for a person's words, actions, and teachings was given birth to. They may claim to know, they may claim to be conduit of something but the moment their words and/or promises do not come to volition they bail out by stated the accepted excuses, *"I am simply a conduit, maybe you are being tested further, maybe you are still not pure enough to understand, maybe you have the bad energy of some other person around you, maybe I misread the tea leaves,"* and the list goes on. But, what the person who claims and/or teaches any form of spirituality does not do is express the truth, *"I am a liar. I am simply doing this to make money, to get what I want out of people, to fix the hole in my psyche where I hope to be something more than nothing and this is the only way I can figure out to do it."*

Here is the fact, a true teacher does not teach. A true teacher does not try to tell you anything. A true teacher steps out of the way and let's you be you, learning what you need to learn in your own time. A true teacher never claims to be anything.

At the root of all problems with this life is the individual desire to be more, to want more, and to feel that they are not good enough in themselves; right here, in the right now. From this, religion was given birth to. From this, all the false profits were given birth to: old and new.

If you can just let go. If you can just be who you are, where you are, and desire nothing more. If you can feel the good and the bad of life and not blame it on the fact that you are not holy enough or that god is testing you; think how free you would be? You would have no need to give any false profit any means to fill the gaping whole in themselves and their own interpersonal psychology which causes them to try to be a teacher, a psychic, a palm reader, a clairvoyant, a priest, or a whatever. Stop financing their lifestyle! Be whole onto yourself.

Life is life, there is going to be good and bad in it. This is your life. That is just the way it is. Everyone's life is the same. Stop looking outside of yourself to religion and false teachers attempting to find a reason and an answer, where there are none. You will pass through your life, receiving and being taken from. This, just like everyone else. You will be happy, and you will be sad. You will be joyous, and you will be angry. No one is perfect. There is no perfect teacher. We are all they same no matter who claims what. They are never what they claim to be. Know this and you are free.

Let go. That is where the truth is born and the place where no teacher or teaching is needed.

Look At Yourself

Whenever a person feels something is lacking in their life, whenever a person feels that they are unhappy with the people and/or the life-situations that continually present themselves in their lives, whenever a person desires something and it is not forthcoming, whenever a person is unfulfilled, unhappy, dissatisfied, or depressed the first thing to do is, *"Look at yourself."*

Life is born from you. Life is born from the thoughts you think, the choices you make, the words you speak, the actions you take, and the things you do. As such, for all life events, either positive or negative, you are the first causation factor.

People try to deny this. In fact, they go to all kinds of lengths to rationalize, justify, and to not take responsibility for the condition of their life. They read books, they go to church, they go to psychotherapists, they get drunk, all with the hope of being able to turn responsibility away from themselves and to blame someone or something else. If there is one commonality in all the personally created badness in the world, it is that people refuse to place blame where blame is due; and that is solely upon yourself.

Every thought you think, every choice you make, every word you speak, everything you do sets a course of events into motion. If your thoughts, choices, words, and actions are kind, nice, loving, and giving, then good things are usually set into motion. If they are the opposite, the opposite occurs.

You set the course for your entire life into motion by what you say and what you do. This is why the Sage very consciously chooses to think and do as little as possible for then with no action is set into motion. Thus, there is no reaction.

People falsely believe that they can say or do

something and there will be no repercussions. They think if they get away with it—if no one hears them or sees them doing it; if they are not caught, then all is fine. But, that is not true. All you do, even if you do it in your secret hiding place, creates an energy. If what you do is detrimental to anything or anybody, in anyway way, then the course of your life's destiny has been sealed—you have set the pathway for your destiny into motion.

It is common that when a person is dissatisfied with something in their life, they lash out. They say and do things that though they may understand is not of the highest mind, they do it anyway. *"I'm venting, okay. That's my right!"* Yet, in these moments of unregulated abandonment bad actions are often taken that have serious consequences.

In fact, many (most) people do all that they do based solely upon a very selfish, self-motivated, mindset of thinking only about themselves and no one else in any given moment in time. Yet, once again, they seek out justification for what they think and what they are doing. But, the fact is, no matter what your justification or your causation factor, your actions have consequences. Those consequences commonly take on the form of your life being lived in less than an ideal manner if you do things that are detrimental to other life.

Some people eventually come to understand that the way they were thinking, what they were saying or doing, is not to the overall benefit of the entire world and from this realization they stop. Some are even so conscious that they try to undo the wrongs they have unleashed, whether these deeds were done to one person or the larger whole. Most people are never so conscious and caring, however. They do what they do and never take the time to look at themselves and try to be understanding that what they are unleashing onto the world is, in fact, negative. Most simply seek and find internal justifications for their thoughts, words, and actions. Yet, they still question why their life is not being lived in the manner that they want it to be lived. Finally, there are those who simply lie about their existence. They lie to others and even to themselves. Yet, when they are alone and left to their own mind all they can do is question why their life is as their life is.

The source of everything arises from you. No matter what your formative years gave you, no matter what you encountered in your adult years, you are the source of all that is occurring in your life. As long as you think wrong, do wrong, damage other people or other things, or do not care about anyone but yourself and how you are encountering life in any given moment, then you will be defined by those thoughts and actions. You are what you create. If you want to know the reason why, look at yourself.

What You Put Out
is What You Get Back

Life is a complex cornucopia of relationships, human interactions, coincidences, and abstract occurrences. Though we try to find a reason for their happenings, we never truly will.

Since the dawn of rising human consciousness people have attempted to articulate a definition that that would place life into a concise set of defined parameters. Certainly, religion has been at the forefront of this process.

As the world grew substantially smaller, a few hundred years ago, the philosophic ideologies of the various cultures came to be much more interactive. From this, a mishmash of understandings has come to haunt all of our minds—especially those of us who seek true-knowledge and an understanding of universe.

The problem with this philosophic mishmash is, however, the source of the philosophic content has been lost. True understanding of a prescribed religious or philosophic understanding can only be truly comprehended by the individual who was born into that culture. Yes, there are those who move to the source point of a philosophy that they hope to follow and truly immerse themselves into it. But, those people are few and far between. Most, simply hear something, believe that it sounds interesting or good, and then go about spouting this information, (or misinformation), to all those they encounter. Whenever they need to find a justification for what is taking place in their life, especially when that, *"Taking place,"* involves the actions of others, they turn to this non-understood philosophic regurgitation.

The fact is, most people do not understand what they are saying. They have heard something from someone else,

162

believed that it sounded good in some misdirected, abstract manner, and then walk down the path of spreading it to the world. This is particularly the case when an individual hopes to sound knowable and present himself or herself as a person of knowledge.

Most people are very self-serving and self-involved. From this is born the mindset of focusing all of their life upon how they are feeling about the way life and/or other people are treating them in any particular point in time. From this, what they spread to the world is the expounding of their own thoughts, opinions, and ideologies about other people and other things. Many times, these words are defined by using some misunderstood philosophic ideology. In some case, these opinions are very well worded, but they are not the truth. Yet, what they say is presented as the truth and this is where all of the world problems of human interaction begin.

This self-involved mindset is particularly the case for those who grew up in an environment where they were not appreciated or nurtured. From this, this style of person developed the very bad habit of instead of looking internally and trying to create and exemplify the positive contributions that they could personally make to the world, they instead spend their life-time focusing on and discussing the acts and actions of others. And, in fact, being held by the emotional responses they receive from people by focusing their life upon the discussion of others. (People love to discuss what others are doing as it takes all focus off of what they are not doing). The actions of a person who bases their life upon this mindset can be small, for example those who hold onto negativity and frequently speak negatively about others, passing their judgments, saying negative things, and spreading rumors. Or, it can be much larger. There are those who spread their opinions to the world.

The problem with encountering life in this fashion is that from this, due to the fact that it is based upon your own opinions and personal appraisals of another person and/or an event, what you say has consequences. What you say and do, due to your personal definitions, set a course of events into motion in your own life, as well as the person you are speaking about. As you have mentioned another person, then you have brought them into your life. You are forever intertwined. Thus, not only have you defined a pathway that you must both walk down together, but you have also become responsible for what happens to that person due to the things you have said or done.

The fact is most people who operate their life from this level of thought do not care. They think only of themselves and if they hurt someone or set a negative course of events into motion in that person's life, they never give it a second thought. They feel they have the right to do so as they think, *"This,"* as that person did, *"That."* But, this is a very selfish and shortsighted place to live your life from. Moreover, it is what sets the future occurrences for your own life into motion. But, most people never think about this, all they think about is how they are feeling about that person or that thing in a particular moment. And, for those who live in a culture where they are allowed to have a free voice, like here in the West, they spill all kinds of falsities, half-truths, opinions, and lies. Yet, at least in their own mind, they believe they are justified in their action. But, are they?

This is where we must once again return to the original premise of this discussion. Once these types of action have occurred; once someone else has set a course of events into motion, people look for answers. They say when someone does something wrong to them or says something bad about them, *"That person will get their karma,"* or *"They are doing the work of the devil and they will be gong to hell for that."* But, why does anybody believe any of this? They believe it because somebody else said it—someone who knew nothing about the true understanding of karma, God, or how the universe works. They are simply grasping at something to make themselves feel better.

For a moment, let's put all of that belief-stuff aside. If you had not heard any of this stuff, if none of that mind-junk was in your brain, then what would you do when somebody did or said something that wronged you? It would probably make you descend into your animal nature and do something physical. So, what we can conclude is that though all this mind-stuff is virtually never understood by the person who speaks of it, what it does do is to keep us from lowering ourselves into a state of combat. So, it is not bad in and of itself.

This being said, think about this… When someone has done or said something that hurt you or damaged your life, where did it all being? Did it begin from you? Did you do something wrong? Probably not. If you did, then it is your fault. But, in most cases, when someone is wronged, it is due to the fact that someone intruded into your life space, your life relationships, your life creations and decided that they had the right to be there. Once there, if they said and/or did anything to set a negative course of events into motion in your life, it is all on them. But, here is the point. They did it! Through their words or their deeds, they set a course of events into motions. And, as stated, due to those actions your lives are now intertwined. From this, the question arises, are they going to be mind-full enough to care and to try to erase the hurt they unleashed? For each person this is different. Some care enough to care. Others do not. Some are so lost in themselves that all they want is for their opinion to be heard or their actions to be seen so that they can fulfill whatever it is that is lacking within themselves.

As stated, most people are very self-serving and self-involved. No matter what philosophic definition you grasp onto in order to make the negative actions of others not hurt as much as they have hurt you, this will only remain in the level of mind-stuff. If you want to look to something to gain a true understanding about why people do what they do, look to their life, look to what they have lived, look to their interpersonal psychology. Though this will not remove the actions they have done or the words they have spoken at least it may provide you with a new understanding of why they did what they did.

Mostly, what you do sets the next course of events into motion in your life and the lives of those you interact with. What you say equals actions and reactions.

What have you said? What have your done? When you have said and done those things were you thinking about yourself or were you thinking about the other person?

The best thing you can do in life is to only say and do good things. If you are upset with someone, be silent. If you love or hate a person never invade their life-space unless you are invited in. What you put out is what you get back.

Be silent, you are free. If you can't be silent then at least never do or say anything that hurts anyone. And, if you already have done something that hurt someone, care enough to undo it.

Remove your desires and your opinions from the equation. What are you left with?

Be more and your life becomes more.

What You Said. What You Should've Said. What You Didn't Say.

Life interactions are based upon communication. We communicate to say what we want, get what we want, express our feelings on a particular subject, and to state our happiness or dissatisfaction with a life-situation or life-event.

Communication is one of the most natural forms of the human experience. We learn to communicate at a very early age. How we communicate, how we express our thoughts and our feelings is initially programmed into us by the way those around us communicate. Generally, we first learn how to express our thoughts, feelings, and desires by the way our parents and our other family members communicate. This is why those individuals who rise out of a loud, boisterous family generally communicate in loud patterns. On the other hand, those who come from a quiet, contemplative family-scape generally are must subtler in their forms of expression and communication.

Once we have had the basic foundations of our communication skills taught to us by our parents and siblings we then move forward and develop our own unique methods of communication guided by our individual personalities. It is quite common to understand that an adult that uses yelling and screaming to express what they are feeling found that as a child they could get want they wanted if they cried and threw a tantrum. On the other hand, if an individual allows people to rant and rave but does not become involved in their confrontational communications it can then easily be understood that they subconsciously learned, early in life, that expressing one's self in this manner does not lead to any desired end. Thus, they remain passive with their communication skills.

In life, we each are provided with the ability to speak

our thoughts. This is, of course, tempered by where we find ourselves in history and to which socioeconomic, political, or religious backdrop we are born.

Once we understand the definition of our communication skills, and which way of communicating is most beneficial and rewarding to our life, we then move forward and say what we say guided by our beliefs, our ego, and our understanding of interpersonal relationships. Some people are very conscious and thoughtful in how they communicate, other are rude, unthinking, and judgmental in all that they say. Who are you? And, are you honest with yourself in the way you communicate and how your communications are interpreted by other people? The fact is, many people are so lost in their exaggerated sense of Self that they do not even take the time to consider how the manner in which they communicate is affecting others that they speak with and/or the world around them as a whole.

In each of our lives we express how we feel—we say what we say. How many times have you said something that you wish you had not said? How many times have you said something that you believed came out wrong? How many times have you, once you have expressed something that you believed came out wrong or was not a correct or righteous expression of your thoughts, did you work to correct what you said? The answer to these questions provides you with deep insight into how you view the world, how you view yourself, and whether or not you have a truly respectful understanding of life and the lives of those that exist around. For, if more times than not you stand firm in what you have said, even if it was hurtful to someone/anyone or anything then this fact alone allows you to peer into yourself and see that you are a very self-centered individual. Moreover, if you do not care how what you have said affects other people and life events, it tells you that you exist in a space of vanity and unaware self-righteousness; sociopathy if you will. From this insight and understanding it allows you, if nothing else, to understand how you perceive this world. It also tells you that you may need to take a look at yourself, how you perceive others, and how you will be remembered because your life is defined through your words and your actions.

Aside from simply what we say, when we communicate, and how we say it, there are times in the midst of conversations when we realize the direction in which the conversation is heading, and we consciously choose to not say what we internally wish to say. This is called, "*Discretion*," and it is one of the highest forms of selfless, interactive human understanding. …You know what you want to say. …You know what you could say is the truth. …But, you choose not to say it because the truth, at least in that particular situation, will only cause the discussion you are involved with to progress towards the realms of negativity.

The thing about human existence is, many people are so lost within their own lying-mind that they do not have the ability to truly look within themselves and to see or care about what effect they are having on others. From this is born the mindset of irrational justification for a person's thoughts, words, and actions. Therefore, to not fall prey to this selfish mindset you can simply employee your own internal sense of discretion. From this conscious action you are left whole and self-aware enough to not have to express what you think in order to make yourself be seen as something more and/or better. This is a true state of self-actualization.

Many interpersonal conversations are based upon one person trying to make their thoughts and their feelings more prominent and more definitive than the other person or persons. But, this is not true interactive conversation. This is ego. And, many people base their entire form of conversation upon attempting to project that they know more, that they are more right than the other person(s) involved in the conversation. I am sure we have all interacted with people like this. But, if we possess enough interpersonal wisdom to not have to prove that our point is the right point then this is where a true understanding of interactive human consciousness comes into play.

This fact is much harder to emulate when you are in a conversation with a person who has or is doing bad things. When they are hurting you and/or other people via their conscious or unconscious actions. Then, the term, *"Bite your tongue,"* really comes into play because though you posses the discretion to not need to win every discussion you enter into, what they are doing is simply wrong, and though you may want to express the truth via your words, your higher self keeps you from doing so.

As is the case with all life, we each rethink what we have done or said once an unsavory situation has occurred. This too is the case with interpersonal conversations, especially when you have been forced to interact with an individual exhibiting lower consciousness by lying, changing the facts, or misrepresenting the truth. *"I should have said...,"* is a common thought when we internalize these conversations after the fact. None-the-less, it is up to you to be more than that person, not fret about what you didn't say, and move on and away from this type of individual as a person like this is their own worst enemy and is setting up the pathway for their own lack of life-fulfillment and self-destruction by not only being dishonest in their words but thereby projecting their own sense of lack of self-awareness to the entire world.

Conversation is at the root of human grown and expanding understandings. It also provides you with a microscope to view into the mind of those you are conversing with.

Know yourself. Know your own mind. Refine your interactive skillset and move forward into the world never spreading falsehood, only speaking your own truth in the most palatable manner possible.

Words lead to actions. What actions do you want to instigate?

Where Does Your Empowerment Come From?

Each person wants to exist in a world where they are liked, loved, well thought of, and even respected. They want to be cared about and they want to have their life mean something. To achieve this, people go to all kinds of lengths. The problem is, these lengths are commonly defined by less than ideal actions. From this, though a person may, at least temporarily gain some of the something they desire, it eventually falls away because it was not a life constructed upon consciousness, thinking of others first, and caring about humanity more than one cares about themselves.

Take a moment and think about the various things you have wanted for your life. Look at what you want now. What are you doing to receive it? But, more importantly, think back to what you wanted one year ago, five years ago, ten years ago. Did you receive those life-things? If so, what was the price of you getting them? How did you getting them affect others? And, once you got them did, they truly make you a better, more whole and happy individual?

This is thing about time; it allows us to gain perspective.

In life, there is one common problem. That problem is, most people think about themselves first. They only care about other people in so much as they affect them. Obviously, this is a very selfish mindset. But, this is how much of the world operates.

Think about this, how many times has someone only been thinking about themselves and your life or your life evolution was negatively affected by their behavior? Now think about this, how many times have you hurt someone else's life by you only thinking about yourself and you did not even care?

Right now, take a moment. Think back one day, one month, one year, or five years—think about another person that you interacted with. Focus on them instead of yourself. Think about how your own self-involved, selfishness affected them. You probably didn't care then. Do you care now?

If you live your entire life based in a space of self-absorption you exist in a very selfish realm of consciousness. The fact is, many people don't care. They justify their actions. *"I am doing this to get that." "People have hurt me so I have the right to hurt them."* But, more then these mentally verbalized excuses; most people are so lost into the realms of the selfish-self that they do not even take the time to take others into consideration. They do what they do. They do what they do and at best they make up justifications and/or excuses for their actions. But, the fact is, the moment another person has entered your life, either by choice or by fate, you are forever intertwined with them. Anything you do that affects them, affects you. And, though you may gain what you want for your life in any given moment by exhibiting bad or selfish behavior, it is that behavior, in and of itself, that will eventually cause you to lose the thing you gained and/or not achieve your ultimate dreams.

Think about life. Think about the people in your life. Think about the people that you actually know; not someone that you have heard about. Think about these people because by looking at them you know what you know; it is not some abstract rumor, thought, or impression. Think about these people. How many of them are truly happy, truly fulfilled, have truly obtained what they have wanted from and for their life? For most of us, when we actually take the time to take a conscious look, we will see that most people are unfilled and have not achieved their whole and compete dreams. This is simply a fact of life.

Again, look at these people. What have they done to get where they wanted to be? In their process whose life did they damage in a small or a large way?

From any damage comes further damage. The damaged go on to damaging others. Why? Because they have been hurt. From this hurt they feel they have the right and/or the need to hurt others. *"It's been done to me."* But, this is biggest excuse that many people employee and the entirely wrong space to live your life from. This is a space of expounding the negative in life; not the positive. If you consciously set about on a path to hurt, by saying bad things or by doing bad things to any other person, your life will forever be defined by those actions. This is why most people never live their life dream. They are held back by their thoughts, words, deeds, and actions.

Many people, however, do not knowingly set out to damage the life of other people. But, they do not take conscious action. They simply do what they do without conscious thought. Is this style of behavior then forgivable because it was not consciously set in motion? No, it is not. For if you go through life lost in your self, locked in your own mind, then by that very thought process you have committed the ultimate sin—you only thought about yourself instead of the great whole.

174

People lie. People cheat. People steal. People deceive. People hurt other people; whether consciously or not. People lie to themselves about what they have done. People justify what they have done. People do all of these things to get what they want. But, if getting what you want involves the damage of anyone or anything you will never truly get what you want. If you do, it will only be very short-lived. And then, you will have had it but will suffer from the losing of it.

If you are not thinking about others first, if you are not putting other people first, you are living your life from a very selfish mind-space. From this, all that is born is disaster. Be more. Care about the other person first. From this, a whole new world of internal achievement is given birth to.

Try it out. See how it feels.

You Can't Give Enlightenment to a Person

You can't give enlightenment to a person. You can want them to be better. You can hope that they will become better. You can point them in the direction of illumination. You can even tell them what they should do to meet nirvana but if they do not take the steps to reach enlightenment on their own, they will never find it.

There are many religious throughout the world, but enlightenment has nothing to do with religion. Enlightenment is about entering into a space of cross-dimensional rightness.

Religions want people to join their conclave. Religion wants people to believe as they do. But, belief is easy. It takes no effort. It takes no action. Enlightenment, on the other hand, witnesses a person consciously letting go of the things that hold them bound to karma. The pathway to illumination witnesses the person not doing things that create karma.

Like I have long said, *"Enlightenment is easy, it's life that's hard."* Yet, very few people get it. Moreover, even less care about it.

The reason life is hard is because there are all of these people doing all of these things that get in the way of other people's pathway to enlightenment. There are all of these people doing all of these things that are solely based on how they view the world, how they view other people, what they want from other people, and how they want the world to be. From this, they not only create all kinds of karma in their own life, but they set about on a path that places roadblocks in the pathway of other people and hinders them from reaching their full potential. Some people even take joy in this. Explain this to them and they will deny it, they will justify their actions, or they simply will not care. Thus, not only do they hinder other people from reaching their highest goals, but they create a barrier from them meeting their own enlightenment.

"Enlightenment is easy, it's life that's hard," and this is the root cause of the problem and why so few people ever reach illumination. Life gets in the way.

There is one person who keeps anyone from reaching enlightenment and that is the person themselves. If you allow other people to do things that keep you from meeting cosmic bliss, if you allow their words or their actions to take control of your mind, then you have allowed them to keep you from encountering your true ultimate nature.

The Bodhisattva Vow details that the true zealot will continue to reincarnate to help humanity until all reach enlightenment. Nice thought, but you cannot feed a person a glass of spiritual emancipation if they are not willing to drink the elixir. Most people are not. They are far too locked up in whatever it is they are thinking about, whatever it is they are desiring, to allow themselves to encountering illumination. Thus, you can't give enlightenment to a person.

So, where dose this leave us? As in all Life Things, it leaves us with you. What do you want? Do you want to touch the divine essence of the all and the everything or do you simply want to be lost to the emotions of the world delivered to you by other people?

"Enlightenment is easy, it's life that's hard."

But, you have to choose to make the choice to focus on the something more rather than meaningless momentary reality if you hope to encounter it.

Reinventing Yourself

Do you ever think about reinventing yourself? Do you ever think about changing who you are? Do you ever ponder doing things differently than the way you always do them?

Most people fall into a pattern fairly early in their late adolescence and/or early adult life. They begin to do things the way they do them and they change very little as they pass through their life. Yes, some people alter a few of their traits here or there but on the whole most people maintain being who they are throughout their life.

Many people, as they become older, find that they are dissatisfied with their life. Perhaps they did not achieve all of the things that they had hoped to achieve when they were younger. Most young people see the future as promising. Though they may not have what they want today, they believe they will achieve it tomorrow. The problem is, for the majority of the world's people, this is not the case. That achievement never happens. From this, many are left dissatisfied with their life.

There is the others side of this, as well, the person who has accomplished some, many, or all of their goals. As they are doing pretty much what they want to do and are receiving the desired admiration from their friends, family, and colleagues, they are fairly content with who and what they are, how they are doing what they are doing, and where they find themselves in life. Why should they reevaluate their life?

There are many motivations as to why a person would reevaluate and change their life. Most people never take the time to truly review where they find themselves in life, however. They make excuses for where they are and what they are doing. But, an excuse is only that, it is just an excuse.

Every now and then you will find someone who takes the bull by the horns and changes. They make a conscious decision, and they redirect their life. They change their trajectory. These people are inspirational. Whether this redirected life change is a major alteration in their career or in the way they emotionally encounter and interact with other people, their change can be an inspiration to us all.

So, here's the question… Who should change their life? Who should reinvent themselves?

Reinvention must be a personal choice and/or realization. For no one can tell you to do anything. If you change for someone else or because someone tells you that you need to change, that change usually is packaged with a lot of resentment and, due to this fact, it rarely lasts.

But, again, who should change their life?

Ask yourself, how do you feel about you? How do you feel about where you are in life? How do you feel about the way in which you interact with others? How do you feel about what you are giving back to the world?

These are tricky questions because of the fact that the successful person may immediately believe that everything with their life is fine. But, is it? If you are successful, are you whole, honest, giving, and complete with yourself? Or, are you simply basing your self-decided okay-ness on the egotistical fact that you are the center of attention?

For the person who finds themselves unfulfilled or unhappy in life, the answer to the questions comes much more easily. *"I want more." "I want to feel better." "I want to be happy."* Okay, what are you going to do about it?

To be a True Person, to be true to yourself, you need to be brutally honest with yourself. You need to define your placement in this reality. You need to not only see yourself as you see yourself, but you need to see yourself as others see you. You need to look at what you truly are and what you are truly giving to the life of other people.

If you want to change, if you feel you need to change, this is the time to change. Set out on a course. First decide that you want to change. Design a pathway, a game plan for your change. Then, make yourself follow that pathway no matter what. Because it is only you who can truly orchestrate any reinvention of yourself and if you do not try wholeheartedly then there is only you to blame.

Your life is defined by what you feel. Your life is defined by what you do. Your life is defined by how others see you. Your life is defined by how you react to others. Your life is defined by how others react to you.

Everything begins with you. Who are you? What are you? What are you doing to become the best you that you can be? If you are doing nothing, you are doing nothing.

If you want to change, if you want to make you a better you, if you want to become the you that you always wanted to be become, begin to do it right now. Decide to change. Decide to become. Design a pathway and reinvent yourself. Stop wasting your Life Time.

The
Zen